LIFE
IN
FRANCE

French texts edited by the same authors

A LA RECHERCHE DU TEMPS PERDU
Selections by Marcel Proust

IONESCO: THREE PLAYS

L'AMANTE ANGLAISE
Marguerite Duras

LIFE IN FRANCE

H. F. BROOKES
&
C. E. FRAENKEL

HEINEMANN
LONDON

Heinemann Educational Books Ltd
LONDON EDINBURGH MELBOURNE AUCKLAND TORONTO
HONG KONG SINGAPORE KUALA LUMPUR
IBADAN NAIROBI JOHANNESBURG
LUSAKA NEW DELHI

ISBN 0 435 37102 9

Published by
Heinemann Educational Books Ltd,
48 Charles Street, London W1X 8AH,
Photoset and printed by Interprint (Malta) Ltd

Contents

List of Maps

List of Illustrations

The publishers gratefully acknowledge permission to reproduce copyright photographs to the holders mentioned in brackets.

Acknowledgements

The authors would like to thank Monsieur Pierre Thollon for his help and advice over gathering together material in France, the librarians of the Maison Française in Oxford for their continued assistance with and interest in the work, and also the publishers for their patience, co-operation and encouragement.

To the reader

Most of the statistics in this book have been taken from the official French government publications of *INSEE*, the *Institut National de la Statistique et des Etudes Economiques*. There are rapid changes in society in the Western world and a time-lag between the collection of data about the changes and the publication of the statistics. So you are urged to try to up-date the information and statistics about life in France given in this book. Hand-outs from the *Service de Presse et d'Information* of the French Embassy will add to anything you may gather from newspapers and magazines.

Het Brookes
Elisabeth Fraenkel

LIFE IN FRANCE

1. Time Off

Fig. 1a.

Fig. 1b.

Fig. 1 *Work is over*
    (a) Leaving the office, Electricité de France, La Défense, Paris.
    (b) End of the day in the hayfield, Département de L'Allier.

Fig. 2a.

Fig. 2b.

Fig. 2c.

Fig. 2d.

Fig. 2 *Time for pleasure*
  (a) Playing *boules*, new housing estate (*grands ensembles*), Nantes.
  (b) Group rehearsing, Maison des Jeunes et de la Culture, Orléans.
  (c) Peace and quiet at home – on the balcony of a flat in the 'Maison Radieuse', Nantes.
  (d) *Terrasse de café*, Paris.

3

Meeting friends

Individuals don't generally spend their spare time according to a set pattern, and neither do nations. What they decide to do depends on the opportunities available. If you want to play tennis but there aren't any courts in your district, that's just too bad; tennis won't be one of your leisure activities. It obviously works out like that in France, too.

But in France, if you just want to meet your friends – or friend – it is easy. You can drift along to a café and sit at a table outside on the pavement – or terrace as it is called. A good way for boy to meet girl.

If the weather is really cold or you want to liven up the scene with some music on the juke-box you can always go inside, but generally it's more fun on the *café terrasse*, and the French climate is kind.

There are literally thousands of cafés in France. It has to be a very small village not to have a single one. If there is only one café, young and old frequent it, enjoying a drink and a chat, but they don't get in each other's way. If there are several cafés, the young often make one café fashionable for some time until they get bored and move off to another.

The *café terrasse* has the advantage of being open to passers-by. If a friend walks by, you give him – or her – a shout and a wave. He comes to join you at your table, not necessarily to sit down if he hasn't the time, but long enough to be matey and exchange news.

Sitting at his table on the terrace the French boy can wait for his girl-friend or she for him, and they can stay for an hour or longer, drinking coffee, sipping a soft drink, like an orange squash or a *sirop* (which is rather sweet), or a *Gini*, a bitter lemon (without the gin). Or they might order a lager beer, either *une bouteille* or *une pression* on tap. Or maybe, the 'hard stuff', like whisky or absinthe if they can afford it. They won't be pressed to order another.

A rendezvous or a chance meeting is not everybody's idea of fun, so some members of the French younger generation join *une bande* – a gang – which makes a particular café its headquarters.

Transport

A special feature of the French scene that helps young people in France to enjoy their time off is the large number of motor-scooters, mopeds, and motor-bikes they own. A *moto* or a *bécane* certainly helps you to get around, and it's cheap to run. You will see and hear them all over France in town and country alike. It is becoming the done thing to try to earn enough money to buy a moped and roam the countryside either in groups or alone or with a friend on the pillion. There are young men with high-powered motor-bikes about, but they seem on the whole to be sporting specialists. Mopeds are – universal.

If you are lucky, in well-paid work, or have indulgent parents, then the car is the thing.

4

Fig. 3 Brand new!

Fig. 4 Citroën Deux Chevaux.

Fig. 5 *Dans la Renault 16 on est bien chez soi.*

Fig. 6 Peugeot 304.

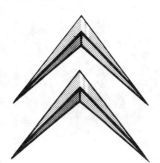

Fig. 7 The car symbols.

Whatever the form of transport, the chances are that you will end up sitting happily on the *café terrasse*, relaxing with your friends.

Types of vehicle

Une totale liberté de vous déplacer en toute indépendance

Name	Engine capacity	Remarks
Un cyclomoteur	under 50 cc	No driving licence or test. Permitted age 14.
Une motocyclette	over 50 cc	Driving licence and test required. Permitted age 16. Referred to as *la moto*.

Both types are often called *la bécane* from the trade name of the French firm MOTOBÉCANE, which has enormous sales in France.

Une voiture	a car of any size	Driving licence and test. Permitted age 18. Sometimes referred to as *la bagnole*.

The cinema

Time off needs a change of scene from time to time. Hanging about cafés, mouching round the streets, is cheap enough, but sitting in the cinema has its attractions. In France members of the younger generation form the majority of the cinema audience. Of course it depends where you live as to whether you have a cinema to go to. In France, as in other Western countries, there is a tendency for cinemas to be shut down. But Paris is well provided with cinemas, and boasts more than a quarter of all French cinema-goers; there is a wide choice of films to see. In the country places of entertainment are in any case fewer, and they are diminishing.

But the cinema and the film industry are considered important in France. There is the government-sponsored *Centre National de la Cinématographie*, and since 1953 government loans have been provided for film-making and for opening a cinema in a new housing development.

Fig. 8 No good queuing for this film if you're under 13.

6

The kind of films young people in France prefer won't surprise you – *les Westerns, les thrillers,* musicals, American situation comedies, films of adventure and horror. Naturally the French have their favourite film-stars, and any number of magazines (see p. 117) which publish life-stories and pull-out pin-up photos of the idols of the day. The stars are not all French, of course, but if you read a magazine of the moment you will probably find at least one current French-born favourite. France attracts international film-stars, who seem to like working and living there. You will often find a serious article or an interview with a famous French film director in an otherwise rather light-hearted magazine. You will find references to revivals of interesting old films.

Short list of old 'classic' films which are sometimes revived, with the names of their directors

René Clair   *Les Grandes Manoeuvres*
                 Sous les Toits de Paris
Marcel Carné   *Les Enfants du Paradis*
Jean Renoir   *La Règle du Jeu*
                 La Grande Illusion

Newer 'classic' films

Alain Resnais   *Hiroshima mon Amour*
                   L'Année dernière à Marienbad
François Truffaut   *Les Quatre Cent Coups*
                       Jules et Jim
Jean-Luc Godard   *A bout de souffle*
                     Vivre sa vie
Jacques Tati   *Les Vacances de M. Hulot*
                  Mon Oncle
                  Jour de fête

The French take the cinema seriously. Perhaps that is why there are so many *Ciné-Clubs* in France, 12,000 in 1969. Questionnaires sent out to secondary-school and university students in 1971, however, revealed that only 40 per cent of ciné-club members were interested in the films shown by the clubs; 36 per cent joined for the sake of the companionship. The cinema seems to provide a focus for the young, and to be associated in their minds with *la sortie avec les amis.*

As the result of findings like these the French have great plans for creating what they call *complexes de loisirs* or *unités de loisirs*; on a single site you will be able to see a film, have a drink at a bar and end up in the dance-hall – *le dancing.* In Paris there are some very expensive 'fun palaces' of this kind, but it will take a long time before they are available for those who are short of money.

7

Fig. 9 Maison de la Culture, Thonon, Haute-Savoie.

Pop music

Young people in France are as likely to go to pop concerts or keep a background of pop music going on the radio as anyone else. Pop stars flourish and fade away in popularity in France as in any other country, so it would be absurd to try to list current pop idols or the discs they have made. However, there is a special and continuing tradition in France of singers who perform particularly in Paris cafés and music-halls. They can be noted for their moving, sometimes sentimental songs, for their political 'bite', or for both. Names to be reckoned with are the late Edith Piaf, Yves Montand, and Georges Brassens. The *chanteurs* and *chanteuses* often write their own words and music.

In some large towns the government has helped to found a *Maison de la Culture*. The Ministry of Culture has oversight over these cultural centres, which are for the whole community, not specially the young. But a centre may have a cinema, one or two theatres (about the only place the live theatre can get a look-in in the provinces), a concert-hall, a disco-thèque, a library, exhibition galleries and lecture rooms for such things as public lectures on scientific topics. So there is plenty going on for young people to choose from at a centre.

A *Maison de la Culture* almost always has a cafeteria, which is a great attraction. They try to keep the whole place open all day and make it informal and friendly, with as few rules and regulations as possible. You won't see many notices of *Défense de* . . . on the walls.

Youth clubs

France has its Youth Clubs, too, run by the *Ministère de la Jeunesse et du Sport*. They get additional financial help from the local authorities for equipment and running expenses. A *Maison des Jeunes* – its title often includes *et de la Culture* or *et des Loisirs* – or a *Club de Jeunes* has a director and one or two *animateurs*, leaders whose job it is to make things 'go'. But youth clubs are not all that popular. Many boys and girls prefer to form their own gang of *copains* (mates). The club is too official or

Fig. 10 Maison des Jeunes et des Loisirs, Cachan, Val-de-Marne.

institutional for them, too much like school. But it may be better than nothing if you want a change of scene. At one club a boy of twenty told an enquirer: 'It's bloody boring here but less so than other places.' At least a club provides a games room, possibly judo classes, and also a workshop where you can potter about. It may have a stage for amateur dramatics, and a ciné-club.

LES HAUTS DE BELLEVILLE

MAISON DES JEUNES ET DE LA CULTURE
43, rue du Borrégo - Paris-20ᵉ
Tél. : 636-68-13 C.C.P. Paris 14.999.17

Au plus haut point de Paris,
la Maison ouverte à tous propose...

...A SES ADHÉRENTS, DES ACTIVITÉS

CULTURELLES
ART DRAMATIQUE, BIBLIOTHÈQUE, CINÉ-CLUB, COURS D'ALLEMAND, DANSE CLASSIQUE, DANSE FOLKLORIQUE, DANSE MODERNE, DESSIN D'ART, ÉCHANGES INTERNATIONAUX, GUITARE CLASSIQUE, INFORMATION POLITIQUE ÉCONOMIQUE ET SOCIALE, MUSIQUE CLASSIQUE ET MODERNE, SORTIES SPECTACLES (CONCERTS, THÉATRE, MUSIC-HALL), TÉLÉ-CLUB

PLEIN AIR ET SPORTS
CAMPS, CANOE, SKI, SPÉLÉOLOGIE, VOYAGES, BASKET, HALTÉROPHILIE, HAND, JUDO, NATATION, PING-PONG, TENNIS, VOLLEY, YOGA, GYMN. HARMONIQUE

ATELIERS
AÉROMODÉLISME, PHOTO, RADIO

DES SERVICES
BAR, FOYER D'HÉBERGEMENT, RESTAURANT, CLUB DU JEUDI (garçons de 11 à 15 ans) INFORMATION, HOT'BELLEVILLE-CLUB (JEUX, DISCOTHÈQUE, PISTE DE DANSE) ÉQUIPE ACCUEIL, ACTIVITÉ MONO, COURS DE SECOURISME, ENSEIGNEMENT MÉNAGER

Fig. 11 What goes on in a *Maison des jeunes et de la culture*.

9

It is possible that the character of youth clubs will change, because in the future the young are going to have more say in running the clubs themselves. If a group of over-fifteens has shown initiative and formed a youth group of their own, they may be officially recognized by their local or municipal authority. They must prove that they are capable of running their group activities efficiently. Then they are provided with an adaptable prefabricated club-house, which they have to assemble themselves. They can furnish it exactly as they please. The prefabs are designed for clubs of 100 members. Between 1968 and 1972 the French government provided 2 million francs – say £200,000 – for these club-houses under a programme called *Les 1,000 Clubs*. In fact, the do-it-yourself youth movement met the challenge by getting 1,104 clubs going during its first four years. It is still at it.

Other kinds of clubs

Youth Clubs are also often attached to Catholic or Protestant churches. There is the Boy Scout–Girl Guide Movement too, which has five national organizations with about 350,000 members, and there are junior sections of sports clubs.

Fig. 12 Shall we go to the theatre?

10

More ways of meeting people

Not everyone wants to be organized, or even organize themselves in a club. Going dancing is one of the most popular ways of spending an evening out on one's own, though at the same time it is a good way of meeting people. There is generally *un dancing* within reach, not only in Paris but in the suburbs of towns.

In the country France still seems to have more fun-fairs with bumper-cars and shooting-booths than Britain has now. The fairs move from village to small town and on again, setting up in a frenzy of activity in the main square or somewhere conveniently handy. The noise and bright lights of *la foire* are always an attraction, even if old-fashioned compared with the noise – and dim lights – of the more sophisticated discothèque in a town, to which a French boy might well take his girl-friend.

Clothes

So they are going out for the evening. What clothes are the French couple wearing? Probably much the same as you would be if you were going out. The fashion scene is international, especially for young people. Even the names of the clothes are much the same, though their pronunciation may be different.

English	French
jeans	le jean
pullover	le pull
T-shirt	le T-shirt or Tee shirt
shorts	le short
cardigan	le cardigan
kilt	le kilt écossais

Because Paris has been the centre of *haute couture*, and specialist fashion-houses still operate there, some people have the idea that the French are always dressed up to the nines. Well, they aren't, and they couldn't afford it even if they wanted to be.

Casual clothes are more and more the thing. And because there is no school uniform in France the general appearance of the young is very gay and varied nowadays. French people have always had the reputation of knowing how to dress well even if they haven't much money.

Famous names	Often also produce	Often market
Yves Saint-Laurent	*prêt-à-porter* clothes	scent
Christian Dior	(ready-to-wear)	under their own
Pierre Balmain	which are not exclusive	trade name,
Courrèges	but not cheap either.	head-scarves,
Chanel		accessories.

11

THE COST OF COUTURE-CREATION CLOTHES

Labour costs account for about 33%, social welfare charges for 17%, taxes for 15%, materials for 20% and profit for about 5% of the price of the average couture-creation garment. The latter may take anything from 80 to 150 hours to make. Each collection comprises from 100 to 250 models and can represent more than 10,000 hours of preparatory work.

Girls especially will take endless time and trouble when shopping to get the total 'look' right; taking trouble certainly tells when you are shopping for 'separates' and accessories. You rarely see an over-dressed French girl. She prefers the effect of classic simplicity.

In France as elsewhere some of the young hope to demonstrate by their dress and appearance that they have dropped out of the society they were born into. However, there do not seem to be so many 'weirdies' in France as in other Western countries. One thing you are unlikely to see in France is the young 'city gent' with dark suit and rolled umbrella. The young executive does wear a suit, yes, but it is light-weight and usually lightish in colour.

Time off on your own

Not everyone wants to go out whenever they have any spare time. If you live in France and have a room of your own, you are as likely to retreat to it and read or turn on the radio or play your records as you would in any other country.

Time off outdoors

If staying indoors gets boring there are plenty of opportunities to follow a sport in France, whether as player or spectator. It is probably true to say that the French are keener on sport than the British nowadays, at least as far as participating is concerned. And they are keen enough to make it profitable to publish a daily paper devoted to sport, as well as numerous specialist magazines and supplements. From figures published as the result of a survey you can get an idea of how many French people actually do take part in sport.

The French government showed its interest in sport by setting up a Ministry for Youth and Sport in 1968, and by allocating public money for laying out and equipping sports-grounds and swimming-pools. Many small towns and even villages have gone ahead with providing a *stade* for

Fig. 13

This Sporting Life in France, 1970

of 37,800,000 French men and women over 14 years of age

39.4%	never took part in any sport
32.6%	no longer took part
15.1%	took part now and again
12.9%	took part regularly

As you would expect, the figures are different for the young.

Of the population aged 14 to 18

9.4%	never took part
17.2%	no longer took part
17.5%	took part now and again
55.9%	took part regularly

their community. In the country the stadium may only be a fairly rough football pitch. It may have a hut to serve as changing-room and *buvette* from which drinks are sold. But you can often come across country towns in France surprisingly well-provided with *le stade*, *la piscine* and *le camping*, sometimes all grouped together on the edge of the town.

The government provides money to boost sports like rowing and skiing by making grants to the federations of the clubs of the particular sports. It reckons that France will have sufficient sports facilities to satisfy its needs by 1985, according to present plans and spending, so there is still some way to go. But it seems to mean business in boosting sport for at least two reasons:

1. French prestige is at stake when international competitions like the Olympic Games take place.
2. The government has a responsibility for the health of the population, especially of its young people. It has an interest in the physical fitness of industrial workers because they are a vital part of a smooth-running economic system.

As far as prestige in athletics goes, the French government has an uphill task, judging from the 1972 Olympic Games.

Fig. 14 Jean-Claude Killy in action.

Medals gained	Gold	Silver	Bronze
U.S.S.R.	50	27	24
U.S.A.	33	31	27
East Germany	20	23	23
West Germany	13	11	16
Great Britain	4	5	9
France	2	4	7

(In terms of size of population the first two nations in the list are comparable with each other, and the last four.)

In the Winter Olympics France shows up better.
Gold-medallist Jean-Claude Killy, who won all three Alpine ski events in the 1968 Olympics, became one of France's pin-ups, a hero.

The French certainly make the most of their mountain regions, particularly in winter. There is a real rush to the snow slopes during the Christmas holidays – like a Bank Holiday rush to the seaside in Britain.

Winter sports are not so expensive for the French as they are for the British. There are four snow-covered mountain areas to choose from, the Alps, the Pyrenees, the Massif Central, and the Jura. And there is government help for the young: cheap rail fares to travel to the mountains, and cheap hostel accommodation when you arrive.

Solo sport versus team games

On the whole the French are individualists, and this shows up in their sporting preferences. Almost three times as many go in for gymnastics as play football, and nearly twice as many take up swimming as their sport. Swimming is growing in popularity as the number of pools increases, but in international competitions France is still not outstanding. Tennis, too, is quite popular and well reported in the newspapers, but the days when there was a French Women's Singles Champion at Wimbledon are long past: it was between 1919 and 1925 that Mlle Suzanne Lenglen won the title six times.

Le football

Soccer is played in two divisions in France, with the Second Division split into Groups A and B.

Some First-Division Teams in Le Championnat

Nantes	Reims
Nice	Saint-Etienne
Nîmes	
Paris F.C.	

Football has a fair following and matches draw crowds of over 20,000, but there isn't the same football fever as in Britain, nor is there any 'pools' excitement either. International match results show that French football is not high in world class terms – yet.

Amateur football is played with enthusiasm and intense rivalry between local teams in provincial leagues. This is where the municipal and village stadia come into their own.

When you read about matches in the newspapers the number of English footballing terms taken straight into the French language is striking if not surprising; the accounts are easy to understand, apart from headlines like

LES BUTS PLEUVENT
(The goals rain)

Rugby football

At the end of the 1973 International Championship season, *le Tournoi des cinq nations*, the European Rugby-playing nations, England, Scotland, Ireland, Wales, and France, ended up with the same number of points. As far as the rugby union game is concerned, French football is very much to the fore in the international scene.

There are several versions of the story of how rugby football arrived in France. According to one, it was 'imported' by English wine-merchants trading in the Bordeaux area. According to another, it was imported into Le Havre in Normandy in 1880, and from there it spread to the south, to the Midi, taking hold on towns and villages alike. Perhaps because France has made an international reputation in rugby and because the game is a 'natural' as a television spectacle, it is becoming increasingly popular. There are moves afoot to spread the game from its home base in the south and south-west to parts of France like Alsace and Lorraine, so far uninvolved. It looks as if one team game at least, rugby football, has a great future in France.

Some famous French Rugby Clubs playing in regular club competitions

Béziers	
Le Racing Club de Paris	Pau
Brive	Toulon
Tarbes	Nice
Stade Toulousain	St-Jean-de-Luz
Lyon	

Getting away from it all

France is big. Although many French people are worried about the pollution of the environment by industry and road traffic, and about suburbs sprawling out over farm land, there are still vast areas of real unspoilt countryside. So, if you have time to relax, especially at the week-end, there is plenty of space. The French are a nation of campers (see p. 00). If camping can be reckoned a sport then it is one of their national ones. Camping certainly enables the young to get out into the open air and explore their country at minimum cost.

As far as water sports are concerned, canoeing and kayaking exploit some of the swift-flowing rivers. The long French coastline with its numerous small harbours makes sailing a natural sport. But boating can get out of hand in the fashionable areas of the Mediterranean, where the boat 'traffic' is so great during the summer holidays that the authorities have had to issue parking discs giving small boats $1\frac{1}{2}$ hours' 'parking' time at the quayside.

Fishing is a sport that the French really go in for. On a Sunday there won't be a stretch of river or a canal bank without its angler – and the angler won't necessarily be middle-aged either. It is the young men who do the fishing while the girls see to the picnic or simply stay at home. Fishing in France is not so extensively 'preserved' by private owners as it is in Britain. Where a fishing licence is required, you can usually get it easily from the local café or village store.

Fig. 15 *La Chasse* in Sologne.

La chasse is another great French country sport; it means shooting, not hunting in the English sense. It used to be reserved for the aristocrat, the landowner and the farmer but nowadays when you see the notice

CHASSE RÉSERVÉE, or CHASSE GARDÉE,

nailed to a tree or a fence, the shooting rights may be reserved for members of the local community or for a syndicate of town-dwellers.

The date in September when *la chasse* is open is a great day in France. The shop-windows are full of all-weather tasteful clothes for the well-dressed *chasseur*, waterproofed from head to foot. And the china and hardware stores set out a selection of stewpots and casseroles for cooking the game in, decorating their shop-windows with pheasant feathers and stuffed animals.

16

La chasse is so popular that pretty nearly anything that moves (including the human race – accidentally) is shot at. So some restraining influence has had to be placed on the numbers of sportsmen by a government licensing system. And the notice

REPEUPLEMENT

tells the tale that the area is being restocked because it has been denuded of game. *La chasse*, like angling, is not an exclusive sport in France, nor one for the elderly only.

But mountain- and rock-climbing certainly are for the young and active. If you are between 16 and 30 years of age you can get instruction in climbing at one of the eighteen centres in the French Alps or at others in the Pyrenees. The centres are run by the *Union Nationale des Centres Sportifs de Plein Air* (UCPA), with government help.

Then there is potholing and caving. In the Central Pyrenees there are exciting subterranean glaciers and frozen lakes to be explored, and in the Dordogne region of south-west France you get the impression that the area is honeycombed with caves. A *grotte* is often advertised as the local attraction, but it can be disappointing and very commercialized. Prehistoric man, the cave-dweller, would be surprised at the entrance fees charged for viewing his home in the Dordogne, for this is an area where he lived. The pictures he painted on the rock-face of the caves at Lascaux still decorate prehistoric man's underground 'cathedral' or 'art gallery'. Unfortunately visitors will not be allowed in the Lascaux caves until the problem is solved of preventing a mould spreading over the rock-face when people crowd in polluting the air with their breath. But there are many more caves with paintings, and *grottes* with stalagmites and stalactites, to be discovered.

Fig. 16 Prehistoric cave painting, Lascaux.

An outdoor game but not away from it all

A specially French national game or pastime is *boules*, or its modern version *pétanque*. The British might call it a simplified game of bowls. In Britain 'bowls' conjures up a picture of smooth green turf that is almost holy ground, and scarcely to be trodden on except by serious elderly ladies and gentlemen playing a discreet, quiet, canny game. In France you play on any fairly level patch of ground, often on gravel or beaten dusty earth. The pitch can be in the shade of trees surrounding a market-place or a public square; or it can be the wide gravel path between the flower-beds in public gardens, in fact anywhere convenient. Young and old seem to play, and except for the serious games where money is involved or in national competitions, playing *pétanque* is a pretty light-hearted matter. There's a good deal of 'gamesmanship' involved and bumps in the ground only make the game more chancy and interesting.

Fig. 17 *Pétanque*, Esplanade des Invalides, Paris.

It is reckoned that

5 million French men and women play *pétanque* (not nearly as many women play as men).
They have their own pair of *boules* which is all the equipment needed.
A pair of solid metal *boules* costs about £5 and lasts a lifetime.

Fig. 18 Some of the competitors in the *Tour de France* shortly after the start.

Professional cycling

Cycling is another outdoor sport the French are specially interested in, but more as spectators than participants. The race called the *Tour de France*, promoted by the newspapers *L'Équipe* and *Le Parisien Libéré*, brings out the people in town and village as the riders go through the daily stages of the race around France.

The race, an international one, usually begins each year towards the end of June and lasts three weeks. Between 1957 and 1964 a French rider named Anquetil won five times and became a national hero. After that interest waned a bit, but now seems to be reviving. There is a *Tour de France* fever among French people generally, with the radio and television pouring out reports on each lap of the race. All over France small boys tear madly about on their bicycles in dangerous imitation of the heroic competitors. The *Tour* is not the only French professional cycling race; there are others not run in stages. In France cycling is a sport to be reckoned with, to be watched – and taken part in if you're fit enough.

Motor racing

Motor racing is a sport which is obviously far too expensive and too highly organized by the car industry for most young people to take an active

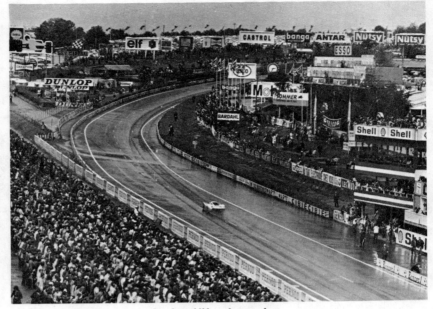

Fig. 19 *Le Mans: la course la plus célèbre du monde.*

part in it. But there is one race which calls for powers of endurance like those of the cyclists in the *Tour de France*, though the motorists' test is shorter in time. Many of the younger generation who are otherwise allergic to television take a keen interest in the Le Mans 24-hour race as shown on the screen, though they might not put themselves out to join the quarter of a million spectators at Le Mans watching the cars hurtling round and round the circuit. It is a strange hypnotizing sight as darkness falls and the cars swoosh past with their headlights blazing. The race goes to the car which does the highest number of kilometres in the twenty-four hours without stopping.

If you've got time off in France there is plenty to choose from to occupy you, plenty that hasn't been mentioned here. Leisure is important, especially in an industrialized society where work can be repetitive and boring and where it is not always easy to find job-satisfaction. But you have to have a base from which to enjoy your leisure. For most people that base is home. So the next thing to consider is the French at home – family life in France.

2. Family Life

It is dangerous to generalize, but it seems that in France the family has always been, and remains, very important in the life of an individual, of no matter what age. The younger generation is looking for greater independence at school and university – even fighting for it. But French children are still closely attached to their parents and immediate small family circle. In addition, the extended family of aunts, uncles and numerous cousins still has to have respectful duty paid to it.

If time has to be spent being sociable in the family circle, there is not much left over for being neighbourly. There are a number of indications that the French family is inward-looking and tries to exclude the outside world: many gardens are surrounded by high walls or hedges, gates are solid and high so that no one can peer in, windows have wooden or metal shutters which are closed at nightfall.

Fig. 20 The private world of home, St. Cloud, Région Parisienne.

Entertaining

The French are not given to dropping in to each other's houses for a cup of tea or coffee. They do not issue invitations on the spur of the moment to 'come along and have a drink this evening'. Guests, apart from members of the family, tend to be rare. They may be asked to a formal tea-party, a meal which French people do not usually indulge in. If guests are in fact invited to a midday or evening meal, it will be an elaborate one which takes hours to prepare. It seems as if the French believe it would be rude to offer everyday family fare to a guest. They are much more likely to take him out to a restaurant.

Women guests in France are not often asked if they would like to take off their coats, tidy their hair or do their make-up in a bedroom in the hostess's house or flat; that too would be judged to be an intrusion. The French have not really got a word for 'spare room' or 'guest room', possibly because guests are not usually asked to stay overnight.

But for members of the family it is different. If you are French, you are more likely to go to stay with members of your family for your holidays than to go anywhere else. You are very likely to go to stay at your grandmother's in the country.

Les séjours de vacances des moins de vingt ans

	5 à 9 ans	10 à 13 ans	14 à 17 ans	18 à 20 ans
Avec les parents:				
En famille	68%	55%	56%	51%
Chez des amis	19%	21%	23%	23%
Sans les parents:				
En colonie de vacances	11%	18%	7%	6%
Ailleurs	2%	6%	14%	20%

Meals

Daily life still follows the traditional pattern. It tends to revolve around meal-times. Breakfast has never been much of a meal in France, because it only consists of a cup or bowl of coffee and a piece of French bread, with or without butter. On Sundays and special occasions you might have delicious crescent-shaped *croissants*, or bun-shaped *brioches*, fetched newly baked from the baker, to eat instead of bread; they are mid-way between a bread roll and a pastry, richly made with butter.

Hardly any family bothers about 'tea' as a meal. Small children probably have their *goûter* during the afternoon because they need to have their energy stoked up more frequently. But the midday and evening meals are really important occasions when members of the family are expected to sit down to table and stay there till the meal is over. And it

Fig. 21 Meal time.

Fig. 22 Taking bread home for the midday meal.

takes a long time for the succession of courses to be eaten and washed down with *vin ordinaire*. The French spend more time and money proportionately on food and drink than most other nations, and their standards are high, even for ordinary everyday meals.

Of course, in a big city like Paris it gets increasingly difficult if you work in the centre to get home for a meal at midday. Factory canteen, school and restaurant meals may have to take the place of the family meal then, but the idea of simply having a snack at midday is only just beginning to catch on. Generally you know when it is 12 noon in France because in factory areas, in the streets of towns and villages, there is a sudden bustle and increase in traffic as people make for home. Then peace descends for two hours or so; the place seems deserted. Even food shops, butchers' and bakers' are closed, while families have their midday meal. Then the rush of traffic starts again – in the opposite direction, back to work.

The long midday break means that French people work later hours and supper does not generally start until 8 o'clock. Supper is even more of a family gathering than the midday meal, and quite small children stay up regularly for it.

Family relationships

French children, rich or poor, have always been used to being with grown-ups. They tend to be brought up exclusively in the close family circle. Play-groups are rare in France; you do not organize your children to play with the neighbourhood children. However, being constantly in the company of adults does not seem to make French children more relaxed with their parents or produce a specially happy relationship between them. On the contrary, parents in France have always claimed the right to exercise strict authority over their children, which naturally leads to tension and often to rebellion.

23

Marriage

In the past parents would influence their children's choice of wife or husband. It was not uncommon for marriages to be arranged by the respective families, and the acquaintance the young people might have with one another before the wedding ceremony might well be limited to a few Sunday afternoon walks taken in full view of the rest of the family, who would be trailing along behind. But France is changing, even if slowly. In a book published in 1966 the author writes: *Le grand changement est que dans le système traditionnel, les jeunes étaient mariés...aujourd'hui ils se marient.* Young people used to be married off, now they just get married.

In former days, when a girl married she lost a good deal of whatever independence she may have had. It was not until 1965 that a bill was passed in the French Parliament allowing a married woman to have her own bank account, and not until 1970 that the law gave her equal rights with her husband to decide on the upbringing of their children, for instance the choice of their schools. By this law the *autorité paternelle* was replaced in the family by the *autorité parentale*.

Changes in family life are not taking place so fast among working-class families, who are more traditionally minded than the middle class in France.

Weddings tend to be family parties all over the world, though sometimes they have some special national characteristics. As far as the actual

Fig. 23 Great day for the family, Coigneur, Seine et Oise.

marriage ceremony is concerned, there is a difference between France and Britain. In France every couple has to be married by the *Maire* in the *Mairie* – the Town Hall. This is the legal ceremony. You can be, and until recently usually were, also married in church or chapel. This second ceremony is not legal, like the civil wedding: it is a religious ceremony conferring the blessing of the Church upon the marriage. More and more young couples in France are dispensing with the religious ceremony, the 'white wedding', the large number of guests, and the special dressing up that goes with it. They are breaking away from the tradition of a family gathering. At the Mairie, which is inescapable, they may have to listen to a homily from the Mayor, reminding them of their civic duties and their responsibilities to their children in the future. But they may duck the sermon in the church.

Many French couples in fact plan their families, in spite of the general attitude of the Catholic Church towards birth control, but they won't have learnt about family planning in school lessons, because sex education is only just being introduced on a limited scale. Abortion was legalized in 1974 though all but the poorest must pay for the operation. Also in 1974 a law was passed making the provision of contraceptives a free service under Social Security regulations and from family planning centres. These reforms were piloted through Parliament by the woman Minister of Health specially appointed for the task by the President.

As in most Western countries, boys and girls in France marry early nowadays. They do not wait till they have completed their training or put a little money by. Once educated and trained, they usually both go out to work. Their home life is quite unlike that of their parents, who keep regular hours, own tidy homes, and go in for formal furnishings. The young want to feel that their home is lived in. The fact that it is small, owing to the housing shortage, and that both husband and wife are at work all day means that it may be untidy. A Frenchman, trying to indicate the attitude that young French people might quite likely adopt to their home, said: *Leur appartement serait rarement en ordre mais son désordre même serait son plus grand charme. Ils s'en occuperaient à peine: Ils y vivraient.* They will soon have all the 'necessities' for modern leisure – radio, record-player, records, tape-recorder, television, paperback books – to provide the right atmosphere.

Young people in France travel more than their parents and go further afield. Couples think nothing of taking their very young children for camping holidays. Increasing contact with foreigners with different attitudes will gradually reduce the overriding importance of the family in French society until it is more like that in neighbouring countries.

3. Housing

Is there a housing shortage in France?

For the young married couple looking for somewhere to live, the difficulties are enormous. Housing is a problem in Western Europe generally, but in France people have put up with bad conditions for so long that there is even more to do to satisfy French housing needs. Sad to say, France's housing stock is one of the oldest in the world.

Out of 16 million dwellings
  6 million were built since 1945,
  but 51 % were built before 1914.

France's housing stock compared with other countries

	France	Germany	U.K.	U.S.A.
Percentage of dwellings constructed				
before 1919	51.5	31	35.5	21
between 1919 and 1945	17.1	20	26.5	29
after 1945	31.4	49	38	50

Like everything else we use, houses wear out in the course of time and have to be replaced. They can be destroyed by some disaster; during the 1939–45 war many houses were destroyed in France by aerial bombardment and by gunfire when the Allied armies were driving the German army out. Whole towns, such as Caen in Normandy, had to be rebuilt after the war.

In modern times people expect better housing and want to be rehoused. As the population of France has increased from under 41 million in 1901 to over 51 million in 1972, there are now many more people to be housed. All these factors combine to produce a housing shortage, in spite of the great efforts which the French have made to overcome it.

Fig. 24 Ruined Caen.

Fig. 25 Rebuilt Caen – the University.

The French and the British have had different ideas in the past – and in part still have – about the kind of housing they expect to live in. They also differ in the ways they are trying to solve their housing problems.

What kind of housing?

City-dwellers in France expect to live in flats. A typical block of flats in Paris might have been built in the 1870s. It is rather dark and heavy in style.

Fig. 26 A typical *concierge*.

As you go in the main door from the street, having pressed the doorbell and waited for the door lock to click open, you will see the *concierge* (or caretaker) peering at you through her window or glass door from her rooms off the hall. She checks the comings and goings in the block of flats, operates the door lock, and is famous as the local gossip.

A French city flat is often appallingly old-fashioned. The French are said to prefer doing without domestic comforts rather than without a car or good-quality food. But the old-fashioned flat often has one advantage; its rent is relatively low.

28

LOCAT.OFFRES

A LOUER
PARIS-LA DEFENSE
IMMEUBLE NEUF
JAMAIS HABITE
avec tél., moquette, s. de bns et
cuis. équipées.
STUDIOS 550 F. GDS STUDIOS
850 F. 2 PIECES 950 à 1.100 F.
3 PIECES 1.500 F.
NOVIM. 775-89-85.

XVe, FRONT DE SEINE.
Tr. bel appart 3 p., nf, moq.,
tél., cuis. éq.. 75 m2, 11e ét.,
park. 1.950 F 033-60-71 mat.

PARLY 4 pces, type 2. 1.500 F
954-60-99.

République. Gd 2 pces avec balc.,
remis à nf, tt cft, tél., 5e ss asc.
720 F mois + ch. 227-61-69-267-
43-60.

PARLY 3 PCES, 1.100 F. COP.
954-63-31.

Rez-de-chauss. 80 m2, grand living,
2 chbres, salle de bains., cuis.
Sol.24-10.

M^o FELIX-FAURE. Immeub. beau
3 p., gd cft, 8e, asc. balcon 1.250 F.-
AMP. 11-24.

Meublées

9e, pr étudte, chbre, coin cuis.,
cft ff., entrée indép. 400 F ch. c. Tél.
285-23-55.

St-Michel, Stud., eau dche, ref. 750.
Tél. 325-50-07.

LOCAT.DEMANDES

J.H., 22 ans, employé I.B.M., référ.,
ch. chbre. - 231-32-46.

2 J.F. Hôtesse Air, ch. stud. ou 2 p.
Paris Sud. MED. 05-13.

J.H. sér. cherche CHBRE.
URGENT. Tél. BAG. 44-51.

J.F. sér. cherche URGENT
CHAMBRE. Tél. AUT. 21-76.

Secrét., sér. référ., ch. chbre ds
appt ou stud. - 742-05-06.

J.H. techn. O.R.T.F., réf., ch. chb.
ind. ou stud. - 273-35-25.

Hôtesse de l'Air ch. stud., cft.
Paris-banl. proche. Laf. 16-31

Key to advertisements

Locat. offres – to Rent
Locat. demandes – Wanted to rent
Meublées – Furnished
À louer – To let
Immeuble – property, house, block of flats
Studio – one-roomed flat with bathroom, etc.

jamais habité – brand new
remis à neuf – remodernised

Key to abbreviations

appart. – appartement – flat
asc – ascenseur – lift
banl. proche – banlieue proche – inner
   suburbs
c – compris – inclusive
cft – confort – modern conveniences,
   mod. cons.
   – grand confort – luxury
ch – cherche – seeks
ch – chauffage – heating
chb./chbre – chambre – room
cuis – cuisine – kitchen
dche – douche – shower
éq – équipé(es) – fitted
ét – étage – story/floor
étudte – étudiante – female student
indép – indépendant(e) – separate
J.F. – jeune fille – girl
J.H. – jeune homme – young man
M^o – Métro – Underground (station)
m^2 – mètres carrés – square metres
moq – moquette – carpeted
nf – neuf – new
p/pces – pièces – rooms

park – parking
pr – pour
réf – référence
rez-de-chauss – rez-de-chaussée – ground-
   floor
sér – sérieux – responsible
s de bns – salle de bains – bathroom
ss – sans
tr – très
tt – tout
XVe – XVe arrondissement – 15th district
   (of Paris)

Fig. 27 Looking for somewhere to live.

Supposing you could not find a suitable flat in town, you might look for a small house, called *un pavillon*, in the suburbs. Until recently France had hardly any town-planning restrictions on the style of individual houses or their siting on building plots. So many suburbs look rather a mess. The French have not been so keen on gardening as the British up till now, and their lack of pride in the surroundings of their houses accentuates the general untidiness.

Fig. 28 Suburban sprawl, *zone pavillonaise*, Villemomble, Seine-St. Denis.

But the French people's idea of what a home should be is changing rapidly, and so is the attitude of the French government to the provision of housing.

It is always easy to find the kind of home you want if you have the money. You can buy luxury houses and flats being built in the most beautiful parts of Paris and in other regions of the country. Near Paris there is a new development called *Elysée Deux*, to indicate that it is as fashionable – and as expensive – as the *Champs Elysées* in the centre of Paris. In 1966 the builders of another new development, *Parly Deux*, wanted to name it *Paris Deux*, but the authorities forbade it.

These kinds of expensive new developments with their show flats, elegantly furnished, offer 'all the luxury of modern living' – tennis courts, swimming pools, cinemas, sauna baths. Everything is calculated to attract the couple who feel they are 'on the way up', comfortably off now and hoping to become richer. Because France has done well in the last twenty years, managers, young executives and professional men in particular can enjoy prosperity and show the world that they personally are doing well by acquiring material possessions and smart homes. This is part of modern France.

Fig. 29 H.L.M. development near Paris.

Subsidized housing

But most people are not so wealthy. A French family of limited means gets a
roof over its head through one of the subsidized housing schemes which
are available. The family might try first to get an *H.L.M. – une Habitation
à Loyer Modéré* – to rent, and claim a housing allowance. Possibly they
might even buy an *H.L.M.* if they could afford it, or if they could get a
government grant of one kind or another; either a grant or a loan, or an
allowance on the interest on the loan, or simply a straight housing allowance. They may in certain circumstances be able to add a municipal
housing grant to the government one. It is all very complicated because
the money is provided by so many different agencies, according to whether
you are buying or renting, and whether the property is public or private.

There seems to be greater concern in France than in Britain to give help
to some categories of people particularly likely to need it. By a law of 1971,
for instance, the French government extended the grant of housing allowances to

persons over 65 years,
to the sick and handicapped,
to young workers under 25.

The law came into force in 1972, and was designed particularly to assist
the most underprivileged sections of the community.

The nearest British equivalent to the French government subsidized
H.L.M.s are the council housing estates, but there are fewer council

houses than *H.L.M.s.* There are whole districts in Paris and provincial towns consisting of *H.L.M.s*, not just a group of tower blocks of flats. The style of some of the districts is rather monotonous, but at least they provide decent living accommodation.

H.L.M. has entered the French language in popular use as a word in its own right, pronounced *achélème*, and increasingly masculine in gender. French people speak about *un achélème* without always remembering what the three letters stand for; but they know that the word means 'a subsidized dwelling'.

Meanwhile the housing shortage continues, in spite of efforts to improve the situation:

Number of new dwellings completed

1961	316,000
1971	475,700

More building has been allowed for in the current development plan, the Sixth National Plan for the years 1971–75. France plans to build an average of 510,000 dwellings a year, an increase of 21 per cent compared with the previous five years. The plan also proposes the renovation of 250,000 old houses and flats, an increase of 34 per cent.

Amenities

The standard of equipment, services and comfort in French homes can be very low: even running water can be a luxury. It has often been said – by the French themselves – that in France people do not worry about the plumbing, whereas Americans and other northern Europeans expect to have private bathrooms and indoor lavatories in all hotels and houses. The need to modernize French houses and flats is shown by these figures:

In 1968

38%	of the French nation lived in overcrowded conditions.
9%	had no running water.
48%	had no private lavatory.
53%	had no bath or shower.
63%	had no central heating.

Foreigners visiting a café in France and asking for the 'toilet' are sometimes shocked to find a 'stand up' lavatory (it has no seat) which is for the use of both men and women, though such a lavatory is hygienic in so far as it usually has continuously flushing water. A lavatory is called *les toilettes*, or *un W.C.* or *un water*. *Un lavabo* is just a cloakroom for washing one's hands.

In recent years, with government assistance, most hotels in France have been well modernized, so you can generally get a room with bath or *bain-douche* (shower) and toilet. And however poor the plumbing in French homes has been in the past, modernization is now making great strides forward.

Fig. 30 A *bidonville* in the suburbs of St. Denis, Paris.

Shanty towns

If you are a poorly paid French worker, a foreign worker without any capital, or an immigrant, you and your family may have to find shelter in a *bidonville*. France is not the only country where there are shanty towns on the outskirts of large cities; in South America there are many. Here is a definition of *bidonville*: *Habitat groupé, précaire, mais 'spontané', c'est à dire construit par l'habitant et non par les pouvoirs publics.* The shacks are built of empty oil-drums or petrol-cans (*bidon* = drum, can), cardboard, corrugated iron and abandoned cars, vans and caravans. Apart from refugees from Algeria in the late 'fifties and foreign workers in the 'sixties, French families themselves have had to resort increasingly to living in shanty towns: between 1966 and 1970 the proportion of native French people to foreigners living in *bidonvilles* rose from 20 per cent to 35 per cent. In March 1970 it was 27 per cent in Paris and 46 per cent in the provinces.

The French are much concerned about the shocking conditions in which the inhabitants of shanty towns live. The government promised to re-house all shanty-town dwellers by the end of 1972, but this proved impossible. For one thing it is unrealistic to expect everybody accustomed to what is in effect camp life to adjust immediately to life in a purpose-built flat. So France has experimented with and is continuing to build *cités de transit*, where social workers help families to settle into a new way of life. How long the ex-*bidonville* families stay in a *cité de transit* depends on how they adapt to new surroundings; some prefer the close contacts and greater neighbourliness of the shanty towns. The French government envisages building such cities to house 80 to 100 families for up to two years to allow them to adjust to 'civilized' surroundings. By the end of 1975 they plan to have 50,000 'intermediate' dwellings, but there will be some families who take longer to adjust and they are housed in *cités de promotion familiale*, each designed for about thirty families. 10,000 of these dwellings are planned for 1971–75.

When individuals or families are judged ready to be moved into ordinary houses they often encounter further difficulty. Local councils and *H.L.M.* officers (Municipal Housing Managers) are sometimes unwilling to accept more than a certain percentage of former slum-dwellers, be they foreigners or Frenchmen, on their housing lists.

There is an awareness of the human misery resulting from living in the terrible conditions of the *bidonvilles*, but no voluntary association comparable in size or influence with 'Shelter' exists in France. Indeed, voluntary and charitable associations are rare in that country.

Meanwhile, those who can afford it are more and more inclined to buy a *résidence secondaire*, either a country or seaside cottage – *un pavillon* – or a luxury villa on the Côte d'Azur in the south of France.

What kind of housing is available varies, then, from the wretched to the luxurious. Where the French live is the next thing to be considered.

4. Where the French live

The Paris of the Parisians

Forget about Paris, the city of tourists; tourists are here today and gone tomorrow. Forget about the sights and the tourist maps for the moment. Map I shows another Paris, a metropolis where the residents and the workers live (p. 36).

The census of 1968 reveals whereabouts in the city they live.

The Population of Paris

Living in Inner Paris	2,607,625
Inner suburbs (Proche Banlieue)	3,000,000
Outer suburbs (Grande Banlieue)	2,600,000
Greater Paris (L'agglomération parisienne)	8,200,000

The Population of France – January 1974   52,340,000

Compared with the total population of France, Paris is very big indeed. In 1947 a book was published with the title *Paris et le désert français*. This may have been an exaggerated description, suggesting an over-populated oasis in an underpopulated deserted countryside, but the description has stuck. Compare the population of Paris with those of the four towns next in size:

Paris	8,200,000
Lyon	1,075,000
Marseille	965,000
Lille	882,000
Bordeaux	555,000

Un Français sur six réside à Paris.
Un Français sur cinq y travaille.

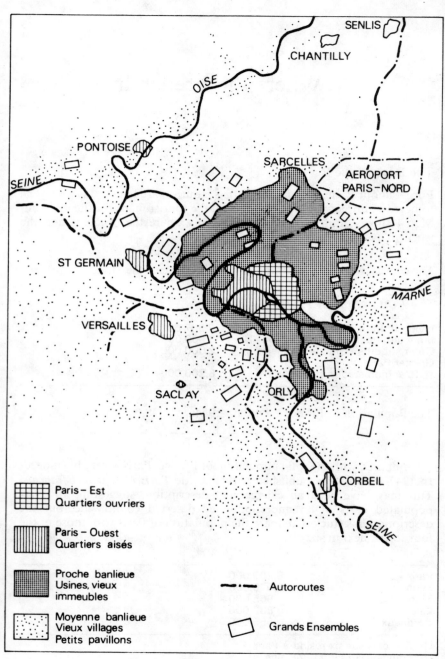

Map 1 Paris and its suburbs

If you look at the small central area of Paris on Map I you will see two distinct districts marked, the one with squares, the other with vertical lines. They represent the poorer and the wealthier districts. As in most capitals, for example London and Rome, the poorer working-class district lies towards the east. Why should the 'West End' be considered more attractive than the 'East End', and its property have a higher value? In Paris one explanation may be that in earlier times the eastern sectors were more liable to flooding from the river Seine; the risk of flooding in the 'East End' made property less desirable and therefore cheaper.

The character of the district remained and was even accentuated by some ruthless nineteenth-century town planning carried out by Haussmann (see p. 50) in the centre of Paris. Haussmann drove his new wide streets – the boulevards – through built-up areas. Old houses were torn down and their owners evicted. They were paid some compensation but, as often happens today, they could not afford the prices or rents of the new properties. They were forced to find homes and workshops in the cheaper eastern and north-eastern districts.

Fig. 31 Inner city street, Paris.

Fig. 32 Flats on a boulevard in a wealthier district.

So even today there is a sharp contrast between these areas of the inner city of Paris and the west and south-western districts: modest living in the east, elegant sophistication in the west. It is a kind of segregation of the poor from the rich.

We tend to forget that Paris is an industrial city as well as the administrative capital of France. Heavy industries like steel and chemicals are mostly located in the northern suburbs, but there are mixed residential and factory areas all round its edges.

Big cities do not usually look their best on their outskirts, especially if seen from a railway train whose destination is one of the central stations. Nor do they look so grand from a car or bus being driven through the suburbs. No matter from which direction you approach the capital of France, you get an impression of almost complete absence of planning. The outskirts of Paris present a messy picture of *des paysages désordonnés* – untidy landscapes – as one Frenchman put it. As you come into Paris you see a jumble of refuse dumps, piles of scrap metal, railway marshalling-yards, army barracks, gas-works, power stations, cheek by jowl with hospitals, alms-houses and cemeteries. And scattered higgledy-piggledy over this landscape are the most varied forms of human habitation, ranging from prim little red-roofed *pavillons* – the relatively cheap small detached houses – to single blocks of high-rise flats apparently dumped down haphazardly to cope with housing a rapidly growing population.

Through these unplanned suburbs the motorways carve their way.

Fig. 33 Hard to remember where you live in this concrete wilderness, Sarcelles, Région Parisienne.

Fig. 34 At Courcelles new estate, the planners have learnt from past mistakes. Gif-sur-Yvette (Vallée de Chevreuse), Essone.

It is only fairly recently that Parisians have had a chance to find out what living on a large new estate is like. In French such developments are called *grands ensembles*, and they are much talked about. One of them, *Sarcelles*, has become a byword for all that can be depressing about a vast development, but French planners have learnt from the Sarcelles experience.

Some *grands ensembles* were planned as new towns independent of Paris, but hardly any of the original ones provided enough work for their occupants, so they have mostly become dormitory towns, *des communes dortoirs*. The result is that thousands of Parisians have to spend hours every day travelling to work by car, bus, underground or train, and often have to use more than one mode of transport. But Parisians are not alone in this.

Here is a Parisian's summing up of life today –

métro – boulot – marmot – dodo tube – job – kids – bye-byes	'If this slogan doesn't beat out the rhythm of your working life, you are a lucky man.'

The Paris transport system

Everybody moans nowadays about the traffic, especially if they live in a large town, and in each town the citizens imagine that their traffic problem is the worst in the world. But most people can consider themselves lucky not to have to cope with Paris traffic. The French crack endless jokes about the chaos in the city in order to relieve their feelings.

Why is there such traffic chaos? Here are some reasons.

The percentage of French people owning cars is one of the highest in the world, only surpassed by those of the USA and Sweden.
The number of private cars on the roads is particularly high in Paris.
French people consider the car is a status symbol as much as a means of transport.
French people claim that the roads belong to the citizens.
French people feel they have the right to park on the pavement if there is no room in the road.
Since the roadway – and pavement – are public property, car-drivers, they think, should not have to pay for parking.
So, parking meters, where provided, are not much used.
Spacious new car-parks are not filled up.
Fines are paid under protest, if at all.

In an interview in October 1972, two high-ranking police officials described how they had tried to discipline parking offenders. The police would put a special locking device on cars parked in an unauthorized place, but the resourceful Parisians soon found ways of picking the lock with hair-pins or paper-clips. If the Paris police towed wrongly parked cars away, as soon as they drove off with the offending car, another one quickly nipped into the empty space, having waited for the bustle to subside.

It is not much use trying to persuade the wealthier citizens to leave their cars at home or on the outskirts of Paris and travel by taxi. In theory there are plenty of taxis, but in practice they are scarcer than in New York or London. John Ardagh says in his book *The New France*:

... a thousand stay locked up in their Paris garages each day for lack of drivers. Strange but understandable when you realise that the taxi-men operate a 'closed shop' into which new recruits can only buy their way by paying for the licence behind the scenes when a taxi driver dies or retires. In London or New York it is said that taxis drive their clients to their destination; in Paris you accompany the chauffeur towards his garage or his restaurant.

This is a reference to the fact that taxi-men behave like most other French people and insist on the ritual of long meal-breaks at midday and in the evening.

If you can't find a cab, or if you haven't the money for a taxi fare, you can try the Paris bus service, which is quite good except at peak hours, when there are traffic jams and chaos reigns supreme. As might be expected, there is no lane-discipline. Drivers inch their vehicles into the smallest spaces in the traffic, whether to the right or the left of the car in front, jamming the traffic even tighter. Suddenly one frustrated driver will start to blow his horn – in spite of a law against it – and then all hell is let loose as others follow suit. Perhaps it lowers the blood pressure, if nothing else.

Fig. 35 Entrance to the Métro, Blanche Station, Montmartre.

The Underground, *le Métropolitain*, is generally the quickest form of transport in Paris. It is called *le Métro* for short. The network of lines is such that you are usually within easy walking distance of a *Métro* station. Underground travel is cheap in some ways because there is a one-price fare for all journeys within the city boundary. Foreigners sometimes complain that what seats there are in the *Métro* trains are hard and uncomfortable, but Parisians seem to prefer it that way.

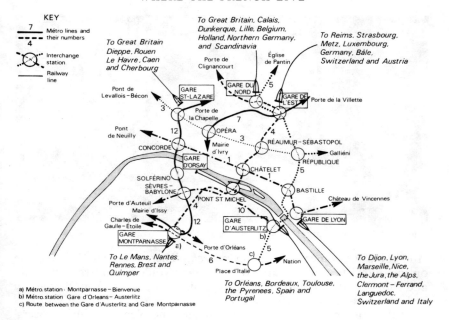

Map 2 Connections by Métro between the main railway stations

There have been some new developments in the *Métro* system. Some very impressive new Underground stations have been built, and a new fast line now connects the centre with the fashionable western outskirts of the city. It is part of the planned *R.E.R.* system (*Réseau Express Régional*). There are plans too for new direct links between the outer suburbs – *un Réseau Banlieue-Banlieue* – so that people will no longer have to go into the centre and out again to get from one outlying suburb to another.

Shopping in Paris

The centre of a city always has its attractions, especially for those living in the suburbs who like going on a shopping spree. Big department stores, *les Grands Magasins*, like *Le Printemps* and *Les Galeries Lafayette*, are famous for their displays of elegant clothes and goods. But not everything is expensive. The stores always have special tables or stalls just outside the shop-front, where they sell bargains; sometimes they are simply cheap lines, sometimes things reduced in price – *Soldes*. It is like a permanent 'Sale' (see top of p. 42).

The shopping scene in Paris is gradually being infiltrated by 'self-service' shops – *libre service* in French. You may find a shop called 'the Drugstore' (complete with snack bar), a word imported from the U.S.A.

41

Fig. 36 A bargain counter outside a Paris Store.

And you often come across a *Supermarché*. There is even a *Hypermarché* on the outskirts of some large towns, where you can park the car easily and shop for almost all the things a family could need, from biscuits to beds and meat to motor-bikes.

At the other end of the scale you can still find plenty of small grocers' shops, corner stores, in the narrow streets of the old section of Paris. The local shops are open late, and you can often see regular customers from the neighbourhood popping in to do some last-minute shopping for supper at 8 o'clock, or perhaps on Sunday morning after church.

Many Parisians do their shopping for Sunday dinner (and for Monday, too, when most shops are shut) at one of the many Sunday-morning markets. Here you can buy anything from meat, vegetables and fruit to cheese, clothing and shoes. You never saw so many pairs of shoes in your life as in a French market: who could possibly buy them all remains a total mystery. Markets are held right in the centre of Paris. They probably retain their popularity because there is a wide choice of goods and the foodstuff looks so fresh. The French are fussy about food being fresh, and still tend to regard frozen food and deep freezers with suspicion.

The custom in France has always been to get your bread fresh every day, so the bakers are open on Sunday mornings, and the cake shops too. Many families still have a habit of calling in at the 'pâtisserie' on their way home from mass, the Roman Catholic church service. Or if they are not church-goers, they may call in on their way home from market to buy a flan or tart – either sweet or savoury – for Sunday dinner.

Places of entertainment are open on Sunday, so the streets of Paris can look very lively if there are theatres or cinemas in the neighbourhood or a sporting fixture on. Otherwise Paris, like any other large town, looks dead on a Sunday.

Fig. 37 A market in a western suburb of Paris.

Tourist Paris

Have a look at Map 2, the tourist map of Paris. You will see that it is divided by the river Seine.

Tourist Paris lies in a fairly compact area; it is not too exhausting to cover it on foot. The sights are located either in the northern district on the right bank of the Seine – *la rive droite* – or on the southern left bank – *la rive gauche*. Each has its own 'flavour'.

This is how a Frenchman listed the different things you would find in the two districts:

> Sur la rive droite de la Seine:–
> les organes principaux du grand commerce parisien: les grandes banques, la plupart des Grands Magasins.
> les théâtres et les grands cinémas.
> le commerce de luxe [e.g. fashion houses, scent, jewellery].
> quelques organismes politiques ou administratifs: palais de l'Elysée [official residence of the French president].
> le Louvre, les Champs-Elysées, la Place de la Concorde.

> Sur la rive gauche de la Seine:–
> (a) le Quartier Latin, la partie la plus ancienne de Paris.
> la Sorbonne [see p. 48] et la plupart des 'Grandes Écoles' [see p. 89].
> de grands lycées célèbres.
> des cafés célèbres.
> (b) le faubourg Saint Germain, le noble faubourg [i.e. 'the aristocratic suburb', as it once was].
> de vieux hôtels aristocratiques [hôtel means 'mansion' here].
> la plupart des ambassades et des ministères.

Map 3 Tourist Paris (see pp. 46–7 for photos illustrating the key numbers)

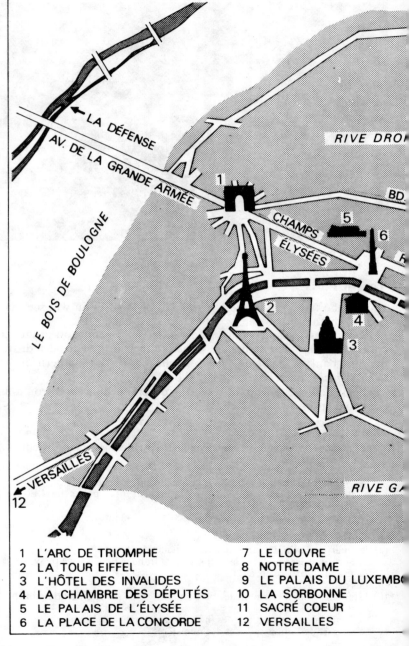

1 L'ARC DE TRIOMPHE
2 LA TOUR EIFFEL
3 L'HÔTEL DES INVALIDES
4 LA CHAMBRE DES DÉPUTÉS
5 LE PALAIS DE L'ÉLYSÉE
6 LA PLACE DE LA CONCORDE

7 LE LOUVRE
8 NOTRE DAME
9 LE PALAIS DU LUXEMBO
10 LA SORBONNE
11 SACRÉ COEUR
12 VERSAILLES

44

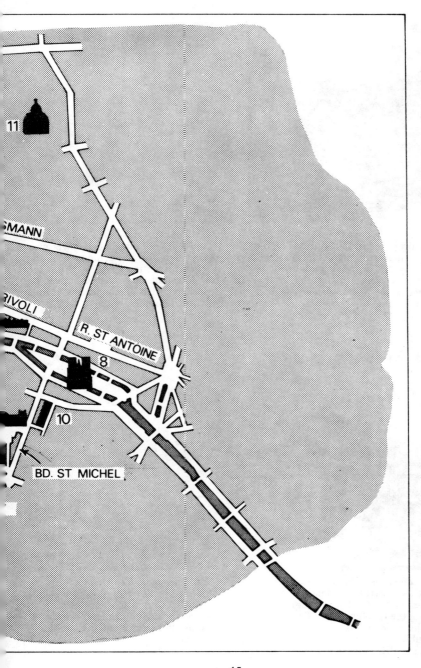

11

SMANN

RIVOLI

R. ST. ANTOINE

8

10

BD. ST. MICHEL

1 *L'Arc de Triomphe*
First projected in 1806 during Napoleon's triumphant campaign. Finished in 1836. After World War I a monument to the dead was placed under the arch – *Le Tombeau du Soldat inconnu* – with its eternal flame.

2 *La Tour Eiffel*
Named in 1889 after the engineer who designed it for the centenary of the French revolution of 1789. From the top, a distant view over 80 km can be seen. Great feat of engineering at time of construction.

5 *Le Palais de l'Elysée*
Built as a private residence (called *Hôtel* at the time) 1718. Taken over by the State during the revolution of 1789. Since 1873 official residence of the President of the Republic (e.g. de Gaulle, Pompidou, Giscard d'Estaing).

6 *La Place de la Concorde*
Designed in 1757. In its centre stands an obelisk (high needle-shaped stone column) brought from Luxor in Egypt. A most impressive square, especially at night.

7 *Le Louvre*
Former royal palace. Building began in 1204, finally finished in the mid-nineteenth century. Now principal national museum of France.

8 *Notre Dame*
Building started in 1160. Work continued for 200 years. The cathedral can be enjoyed as a great work of Gothic architecture, as a monument of an historic period, as an expression of religious feeling, as a timeless artistic achievement.

9 *Le Palais et Jardin du Luxembourg*
The original palace dates from the early seventeenth century. Since the early nineteenth century the home of the Sénat (see p. 121). The gardens are one of the greatest attractions of the *Quartier Latin.*

11 *Sacré Coeur*
Church of the Sacred Heart, built in 1876 as a place of pilgrimage. Standing on a hill, its white imitation byzantine cupolas are visible from many parts of Paris.

12 *Versailles*
Magnificent palace 18 km south east of Paris begun in 1661 by Louis XIV, now a museum. Set in an extensive park with splendid fountains. Includes smaller palaces in the grounds, e.g. *Le Petit Trianon*, Marie Antoinette's charming 'country house'.

47

The Latin Quarter is probably the most free-and-easy part of central Paris to live in, and it is certainly the cheapest. It has been a centre of learning and scholarship ever since Robert de Sorbon, King Louis IX's chaplain, founded the university there in the thirteenth century; that is where the name of the university, la Sorbonne, comes from. Latin was then the language of learning – hence *le Quartier Latin*, where the students used to speak Latin. Though the vast increase in the number of students (in 1971–72 there were about 260,000 in Paris) meant that new satellite universities like Nanterre have had to be set up on the outskirts of Paris, nevertheless students still tend to congregate in the old Latin Quarter. It is a place where the conventions don't matter. And you can sit on the crowded *terrasses des cafés*, at the tables in front of the cafés, arguing and discussing, or simply watching the world go by. Even in winter it is possible to sit outside, for the terraces are sheltered by glass screens and are often heated. The atmosphere is very relaxed.

It has not always been so. In May 1968 some of the bitterest fighting took place in the Latin Quarter when the students rioted, and barricades were thrown across the main thoroughfare of the Quarter, the *Boulevard St. Michel*, called the *Boul Mich* for short.

If you come down the *Boul Mich* from the direction of the Sorbonne you arrive at the river Seine and cross by a bridge to the island in the middle of the river, called *l'Île de la Cité*. Though it is not strictly part of the Latin

Fig. 38 Fishing in the Seine by the Pont-Marie.

48

Quarter the island belongs to it in spirit because the cathedral church of Notre Dame stands here. Notre Dame has survived from the early days of Paris, when the Church and church men used to dominate the life of the old city as they did the Sorbonne.

There is never far to walk to reach a bridge to cross the river. The river banks themselves are generally interesting, especially to the tourist. Traffic on the river is busy with barges, and from time to time boats with sightseers on board go by – the famous *bâteaux mouches*. There always seem to be Parisians with the leisure time to sit on the banks of the Seine below the embankment, fishing and smoking, ever hopeful of a catch, getting away from the stress of life – at least they would if they could ignore the roar of the road traffic hurtling along behind them. A road along the Paris Seine is often called a *quai*, and some parts of these quays are taken over by secondhand booksellers. Their stalls are in fact iron boxes fixed to the parapet along the riverside. The traders are called *bouquinistes*, after the everyday word for a book, *le bouquin*.

Now for the right bank: if you look at Map 2 again you will see a road starting from the Louvre (No. 7 on the map). It is very grand and wide and runs straight for seven kilometres westwards via the place de la Concorde along the Champs Elysées, round – not through – the Arc de Triomphe, and on to a vast new development of the last few years, the replanned *Rond Point de la Défense*.

The same road leads from the Arc de Triomphe to the Bois de Boulogne. It was constructed arrow-straight so that in former times the monarch, members of the aristocracy and the rich property-owning classes could drive in state to the famous wood, with its lakes and restaurants, in search of entertainment.

Starting from the Louvre and going eastwards there is an equally straight road, but it goes through ever poorer districts. It is crossed by another straight road running north–south, of which the Boulevard St. Michel forms a part.

Fig. 39 L'Arc de Triomphe from the air.

Fig. 40 La Défense still under construction.

The name of the man who designed much of this Paris road network is worth remembering because he was one of the first town-planners. He was Georges Haussmann (1809–1891). He was given the authority to demolish houses ruthlessly if they stood in the way of his planned wide straight roads or boulevards, which he proceeded to do. Yet there do not seem to have been any protest demonstrations against his operations. The new highways were intended to ease the flow of traffic – they had traffic problems even in the mid-nineteenth century – but some historians say that the extension of the main west–east highway into the poorer eastern districts was also intended to make it easier for the police and military to put down possible future demonstrations or revolutions; it was intended for *la défense stratégique contre les mouvements populaires*. After all, France had had the most resounding revolution in 1789 and again in 1848; the French have still not forgotten it.

Not all Haussmann's plans were realized during his lifetime, but building continued along the lines he had suggested right up until 1926. Now new town-planners are at work. Sky-scrapers are dwarfing the old buildings of Paris or altering the sky-line, as they do in most other old cities. Argument rages about new developments like la Défense, Maine-Montparnasse or the new University Science Block across the river from Notre Dame. The Maine-Montparnasse building, a new business centre (height 210 metres, 53 storeys), will create a new style of life in the old Montparnasse artists' district. Some 20,000 persons occupy the tower part. Boutiques and shops are located at the base of the tower.

Paris is one of the great capitals of the world where people live and work. It is a beautiful city. It is also a romantic idea, a dream, to people who may never go there. The word 'Paris' may conjure up visions of beautiful

Fig. 41 *Sous les toits de Paris:* the skyline of the most beautiful of cities is changing. Notre Dame's Gothic towers contrast with the modern bulk of the new science university.

fashionable clothes, exotic women, shops, boutiques selling exquisite French scent, accessories, jewellery. Or it may bring to mind painters working away in studios at pictures difficult to interpret, obviously 'modern'. Or it may simply indicate the city where the rich, the famous, the film-stars, exiles from many lands either like to live or where they have found refuge. It has an international as well as a French population.

For French people there is not, nor ever has been, another town in France to touch Paris. It is *the* centre of French life. A famous French writer, Paul Valéry, once wrote:

What distinguishes Paris from all other gigantic cities is that at one and the same time it is the political, literary, scientific, financial, commercial capital of a great nation, and the centre for luxurious and expensive living; and Paris also represents the whole of the nation's past history.

(From *Regards sur le monde actuel*).

Valéry's view of Paris seems to agree with the more modern one quoted earlier: *Paris et le désert français.* But if everything worth while seems to be concentrated in Paris, what on earth must the rest of France be like? Is it really a desert, and if so, what is the French government doing about making the desert bloom?

51

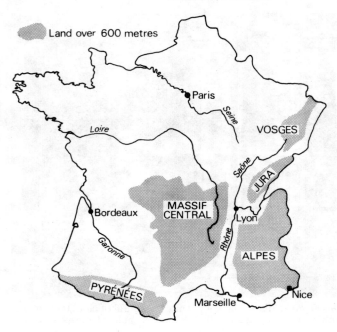

Map 4 France

The regions – some essential geography

The shape of France is easy to remember because it is roughly a square.

France has a very long coastline, so the sea forms much of its boundaries. To the east and south-west there are mountains, as you can see from the map. Only in the north is there a flat plain with no natural boundary.

Here are some important rivers:

Quatre fleuves importants

Nom	Villes sur le fleuve	Le fleuve se jette dans
La Seine	Paris, Rouen, Le Havre	La Manche
La Loire	Orléans, Tours, Nantes	L'Atlantique
La Garonne	Toulouse, Bordeaux	L'Atlantique
Le Rhône	Lyon, Avignon	La Méditerranée

Here are the important mountain ranges:

Cinq montagnes importantes

Nom	Situation en France	Sommet	Hauteur en mètres
Les Alpes	sud-est	Le Mont Blanc	4,807 m.
Les Pyrénées	sud-ouest	Vignemale	3,300 m.
Le Massif Central	centre	Le Mont-Dore	1,886 m.
Le Jura	est	Le Crêt de la Neige	1,723 m.
Les Vosges	est	Hohneck	1,360 m.

Le Mont Blanc est le sommet le plus haut de l'Europe.

There are great differences of climate between the extreme north of France, on the Belgian border, and the extreme south, on the Mediterranean Sea. Here are the three main types of climate in France:

---

maritime   – influenced by the Atlantic Ocean in the west.
continental   – in the centre and east.
mediterranean – in the south.

France has many natural advantages; here are some:

France can, if she wants to, feed her population from the produce of her own soil.

France can produce a great variety of food – and drink – because the climate and soil conditions vary widely over the country as a whole.

The great rivers and modern canal system which is being constructed to link them provide cheap transport. The river Rhône flows fast enough to be harnessed to provide hydro-electric power.

French ports give French industry direct access to raw materials and crude oil, which has to be imported from other continents.

53

France is not rich in minerals like coal and iron ore, but, by co-operating with her neighbours Germany and the Benelux countries (Belgium, Luxembourg and the Netherlands), she can exploit what she *has* got and buy relatively cheaply from the German Ruhr industrial area close to her borders.

France is a beautiful country, but it is not a paradise for all its inhabitants. There are rich and poor districts in the country, just as there are in Paris. Some regions are rich because they are lucky to have something other people want. Other regions have been neglected by France's rulers for centuries. But since the 1950s at last people have begun to think that something should be done for the less fortunate regions, which are all in the western half of the country.

Map 5 La France riche – industrielle
           La France pauvre – agricole

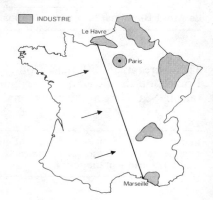

La France riche
> vers 1955
a   66% de la population
     50% du produit agricole
     78% du produit industriel
     72% du revenu national

La France pauvre
> lui envoie ses hommes
beaucoup vers l'industrie

La France riche

On trouve là	les deux tiers* de la population,	*two-thirds
	les trois quarts* de la richesse,	*three-quarters
	tous les grands foyers*	
	industriels,	*large centres
	presque toutes les plus grosses	
	entreprises industrielles ou	
	agricoles,	
	la capitale et son énorme	
	agglomération*,	*built-up area
		around it
	tous les centres d'immigration.	

La France pauvre

Elle ne peut nourrir tous ses habitants,	
semble vouée* à une agriculture vieillotte*	* be sticking to
	* out of date
le niveau* d'instruction y est sensiblement*	* level
plus bas;	* distinctly
les salaires sont plus faibles*	* lower
l'auto y a fait longtemps figure de luxe*.	* has represented
	luxury

In 1973 people were still distinguishing between rich and poor France and between Paris and le *désert français*. The French desert, perhaps, wrote a journalist, but one which feeds the oasis.

Away from Paris

A surprising thing about the regions is the large number of small towns you find there. Even in the more industrial parts of the north and east there are fewer *large* towns than in England. The small towns date from before the industrial revolution when the rural areas were prosperous and needed centres for buying and selling produce. Now these market towns are sleepy and look neglected, with their unpainted house-fronts. They may have a certain old-world charm – at least to the visitor – but if you had to live in one, it might be a different story; perhaps there would be no piped water in your house, no main drains, no 'mod.cons.', though you would probably have electricity. 'Electricité de France', State-owned and operated, is rather enterprising and provides a service even in remote areas.

Fig. 42 Morning shopping in a country town.

The industrial revolution hit Britain early in the nineteenth century. Its factory towns grew quickly. But France lagged behind. Between 1850 and 1950 few French towns grew to any size. People continued to live and work in the country. As late as 1954 more than a quarter of the male working population still worked on the land.

In 1954, out of the total male work force

26.7% worked *on the land*
33.8% worked *in factories*

Factories may produce dirty and overcrowded cities but, generally speaking, 'where there is muck there is brass'. In France the money was in Paris and in only a few industrial centres besides. The regions with their agriculture and small towns were neglected until the mid 1950s, when the French government set about planning regional development. They called it *l'aménagement du territoire'*.

What had happened was that there was a growing drift from the land to the Paris region, where the higher wages of the factory workers and the gay life of the capital attracted the modern Frenchman as a moth to a bright light. So the government aimed to make life in the provinces better and brighter to stop the pressure on Paris. It put a lot of money into subsidizing schemes. It concentrated first on economic development in the regions and then on making the centres of regions into mini-capitals which would provide opportunities for people to relax after working hours.

Here are some of the ways the government set about reorganizing France.

In 1955	Twenty-one new administrative units were formed called *régions économiques*. Each unit provides a big central market for agricultural produce, or it has access to cheap transport for manufactured goods.
In 1966	Eight towns were selected for development as regional capitals, called *métropoles d'équilibre*, to counter the attractions of Paris. They are

Bordeaux   Nancy
Lille   Nantes
Lyon   Strasbourg
Marseille   Toulouse

1 Nord
2 Basse – Normandie
3 Haute – Normandie
4 Picardie
5 Région Parisienne
6 Champagne
7 Lorraine
8 Alsace
9 Bretagne
10 Pays de la Loire
11 Centre
12 Bourgogne
13 Franche – Comté
14 Poitou – Charentes
15 Limousin
16 Auvergne
17 Rhône – Alpes
18 Aquitaine
19 Midi – Pyrénées
20 Languedoc
21 Provence – Côte – d'Azur – Corse

Map 6 French regions and 'métropoles d'équilibre'
Depuis 1790, la France est divisée en départements. En 1955, ces départements ont
été regroupés en 21 régions économiques d'aménagement du territoire.

On top of all this, three whole regions have joined forces to act as one
for development purposes. They are:

Rhône–Alpes
Languedoc–Roussillon } = LE GRAND DELTA
Provence–Côte d'Azur

Le Grand Delta makes up a fifth of the land area of France. Its chief asset
is space in which to expand.

Le Grand Delta est une région d'équilibre de l'Europe.

Like the *métropoles d'équilibre*, the purpose behind it is to counterbalance
the drawing power of the well-established European centres such as
Düsseldorf and the Ruhr in Germany.

How expansion is encouraged

The French government continues to pour money in the regions:

into local authorities for public works like piping new water supplies, or
digging new drainage;
into schemes for irrigating land to grow better crops,
into industry to build factories where there is unemployment,
into the retraining of redundant workers for new jobs in the new factories.

The result is that whole new industrial centres have been constructed
and agricultural areas improved.

Example 1. The Fos-Marseille complex

An industrial development. Fos is about thirty miles west of Marseilles.
A new port is being constructed at Fos, capable of berthing huge 500,000-
ton oil tankers. The port will soon have waterway links with Marseilles,
and eventually via the Rhône river and canal to Lorraine and the river
Rhine.

Heavy industry – for example steel-making and oil-refining – is being
established.

A British plastics plant was built at Fos in 1970.

The industrial zone of Fos is scheduled to be almost as large as the whole
of the city of Paris within the boundaries of the outer boulevards.

By 1985 an estimated 40,000 people will have found jobs in Fos industry.
Add to these the families of the workers, the shop-assistants and people
in the service industries (gas, electricity, repairs, laundries, dry-cleaning,
and so on).

The huge Fos scheme sounds tremendous, but it is being criticized.
The original inhabitants complain of being pushed around. The new
arrivals say that schools and other community buildings aren't ready
when they move in. So people are not entirely satisfied.

Example 2. The Rhône Valley development

The project includes the building of a nuclear reactor at Marcoule,
30 km from Avignon; the canalization of the Rhône so that eventually
there will be a waterway from Fos to the river Rhine for big barge convoys;
and the development of hydro-electric power as the river is controlled
and dammed.

Example 3. The Languedoc–Roussillon development

An area on the Mediterranean coast west of the Rhône delta is being
developed for tourist and leisure activities, with a marina for yachts,
holiday hotels, and also villas and flats for retired folk.

Fig. 43 At the sea-side: la Grande Motte, Montpellier, Hérault.

The provinces are certainly brighter places to live in than they used to be. There is more entertainment in the way of live theatre and music festivals, and the chances of getting a good education and training are better, because universities and technical colleges in the provinces have been enlarged. Provincial newspapers and shops are often of a higher standard than they used to be. There are faster trains and internal air-flights – to and from Paris, of course! But there is still a feeling that life in Paris is a more attractive proposition than life in the provinces.

The government is blamed for poor planning and the piecemeal development of regions, so that in spite of all the public money spent, which after all comes from taxing the people, the opportunities they get in one region don't equal those of some other region. The provincials grumble that developments are too tightly controlled by civil servants in Paris who don't know enough about local conditions. It may be that many parts of the country are still so thinly populated that they simply do not warrant the building of comprehensive schools, for example, or out-patients' clinics. You need a certain number of inhabitants living within a radius of 20 to 25 km, and able to travel in to the centre daily, to make it worth providing such new facilities.

Still, the emptiness of some parts of France is a great blessing compared with conditions in some densely populated countries like England, West Germany – or Japan. France still has possibilities for physical expansion – and for relaxation, too.

Holiday making in the regions

You may be surprised when going through France to find some parts very short of hotels. But you will always find a great variety of well-equipped camping sites, some belonging to clubs whose members have interests in common, for example, under-water exploration, or horse-riding. New purpose-built *villages de vacances* are springing up, designed for families who want a more solid roof than a tent over their heads but one that doesn't cost very much to rent.

At holiday time the French themselves often go to stay with relations in the country, because family ties are close (see p. 21). And the Frenchman is still closely connected with the countryside – possibly only one generation removed from it. Many will have inherited *une petite propriété* in the regions, and spend their holidays there. But, as France grows more affluent and industrialized, its inhabitants prefer to relax by the seaside and, in winter, skiing in the mountains is becoming very popular. Really cheap holidays are on offer to groups of young people.

For the foreign holiday-maker in France there is plenty of opportunity to get off the beaten track. For many visitors the fun consists simply of being somewhere that is so different from home, somewhere where the food and drink, even the times of the meals, are different. It is fun to note how French hotels, beds and bedding, camping rules and traffic regulations, shops and shopping hours, post offices and the telephone system, are not quite the same as at home.

Here are some holiday regions of France, and what they are specially known for:

Region	Special Attraction
La Bretagne	Atlantic coast – beaches and rocks
La Provence La Côte d'Azur	Mediterranean coast – sunshine, colour, Roman remains
La Gironde (Bordeaux area) La Bourgogne Le Rhône La Moselle	Vineyards
Les Alpes Les Pyrénées Les Vosges Le Massif Central	Mountains
La Vallée de la Loire	Castles

Fig. 44 Mont St.-Michel.

Some regions of France in greater detail

La Normandie

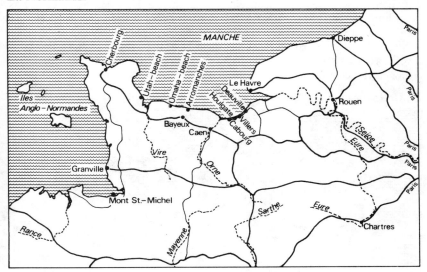

Map 7 La Normandie

Special points to remember about Normandy

Sandy beaches along the Channel coast.
6 June 1944: Allied troops landed on the beaches. This was during World War II, when the invasion of Europe was launched from England to destroy Hitler and the German armies.
Mulberry Harbour near Arromanches: a concrete harbour towed in sections from England and quickly put together; ships then landed supplies for the Allies.
Mont St.-Michel: a monastery built on the summit of a small rocky island, now a tourist attraction.
Rouen: chief city of Normandy. Joan of Arc was burnt at the stake there in 1431.
Bayeux: home of the 'tapestry' which tells the story of William the Conqueror's conquest of England in 1066; it is more correct to call it embroidery on linen.

Normandy is a placid countryside of meadows and apple orchards. It is famous for its cider, its butter, and its cheese; the most widely known cheese is Camembert.

61

The region is being modernized. Motorways have been built between Paris, Rouen and Le Havre, one of the chief ports of France. The railway between these cities has been electrified. In Le Havre a huge area has been laid out for new industries, though at present the fine new concrete roads look a bit lonely running through empty space.

Since the war Normandy has been a favourite region where the city-dwellers of Paris and Rouen might buy a cottage, their *résidence secondaire*, either in the country or beside the sea.

La Bretagne

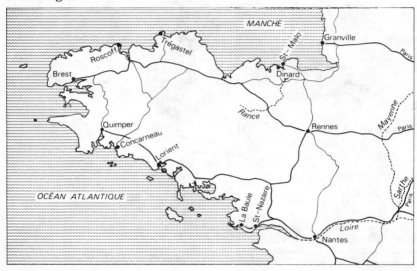

Map 8 La Bretagne

Special points to remember about Brittany:

Splendid coast: varied scenery, high cliffs, jagged rocks, huge Atlantic Ocean waves, small coves and white sandy beaches.
Picturesque fishing harbours: e.g. Concarneau, Lorient.
Traditional folk costume still worn, possibly to please the tourists.
Breton dialect spoken, similar roots to Welsh and Cornish.
Strong influence of the *Catholic Church*; special religious festivals are still kept up, e.g. *les Pardons* – pilgrimages made to ask for forgiveness of sins.
Pancakes: *les crêpes bretonnes* are famous. You can buy packets of them even in Paris.

Brittany and the Bretons have had a hard time. It is a backward part of France, where there are more people than jobs. Families are still large, as though no one had heard of birth control. When there is any modernization, for instance of fishing or of agriculture, it only means fewer jobs for unskilled workers. Brittany is rather cut off from Paris, where the important decisions about investment for the future are made. People speak of *le mur des 400 kilomètres* as though the relatively short distance from Paris was an insurmountable obstacle.

What happens? The young and ambitious leave home for Paris, or, if they still feel the urge to go to sea, for more flourishing ports in other regions. There has been an attempt to settle 15,000 people further south, in Aquitaine, which is thinly populated. And two towns are growing rapidly: Quimper, and Rennes, which now has a university. But Brittany is a problem. The French speak of 'le mal breton' – the Breton sickness: they mean that Brittany is a region that has never really caught up with modern times. Both the agricultural and the industrial revolutions passed it by. It has too many inhabitants trying to make a living in what is a backwater. No wonder the young leave to try their luck elsewhere.

La Vallée de la Loire

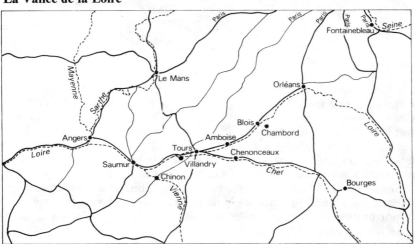

Map 9 La Vallée de la Loire

The valley of the Loire river is often called 'the château country' in the guide books and travel brochures. Of course it welcomes tourists, but it has other sources of income too. It produces early vegetables, fruit, and grapes for wine-making. Because the sides of the valley slope very gently down to the shallow river, catching the sun, the climate is surprisingly mild for such a relatively northerly region.

The country between Orléans and Angers is sometimes called 'the garden of France'. It is a well-watered part of France, as you can see from the number of tributaries of the Loire if you look at the map.

Nowadays the region is crowded with visitors during the holiday season, but it is used to being much visited. In former times the kings of France came to live for long periods in castles they either built from scratch or added to. François I (1494–1547) built the Château de Chambord but he also added a wing to the castle at Amboise, which had been built by Charles VIII (1470–1498).

Fig. 45 Château de Chambord.

Monarchs seemed to like to move about from one residence to another. François I's son, Henri II (1519–1559), made a present of the castle of Chenonceaux – which is built *over* the river Cher, tributary of the Loire – to his mistress, Diane de Poiters. Joan of Arc first met the French king, her sovereign, Charles VII, in 1429 in the castle at Chinon, and put heart into him to fight against the English invaders. You can see that there is plenty of history in the stones of the châteaux of the Loire.

Some of the castles, like Amboise and Blois, dominate the town. Others, like Chambord, are set in magnificent parks which gave splendid opportunities for hunting. Yet others, like Villandry, are set in spick-and-span formal gardens.

If you visit these places in summer you will usually be able to go to the castle during the evening when it is dark and see a performance of 'Son et Lumière'. It is the history of the place told over the loud-speakers in words and music, and visually with spot- and flood-lights which pick out the various parts of the castle referred to in the story, highlighting them. It is certainly a vivid way of putting over history.

The town which is the regional centre, Tours, has always been a place where foreigners go to learn the 'best' French. It is a pleasant city, but nowadays even in France people are not sure if there can be a model of a spoken language. Local accents are more acceptable than they used to be. But the French are still fussy about the purity of the structure of their

Fig. 46 Château de Chenonceaux.

Fig. 47 Château de Villandry.

language and about the new words which inevitably creep into the language, especially English and American ones.

Provence and the Côte d'Azur – Le Midi

If you asked a Yorkshireman 'Where do you come from?' he might answer in a general way, 'From the North'. Similarly a Frenchman from somewhere in the south of France might reply, 'From the Midi'.

More specifically, Provence is the name of a large region in the south and the *Côte d'Azur* is the name of the coastal area – called the 'Blue Coast' because the Mediterranean is always thought of as bright with sunshine and blue waters; people forget that it can be stormy and grey at times. But on the whole they are right to be attracted to Provence, for it has a dry warm climate and a relaxed atmosphere.

During the nineteenth and early twentieth century wealthy people from all over the world came to the Riviera (to give the coast its English name). They either settled there or paid long visits. Since the idle rich had to have some amusements, casinos for gambling, race-tracks, and

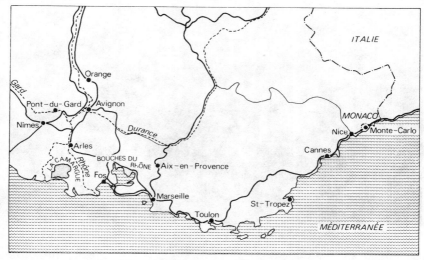

Map 10 Provence and the Côte d'Azur

harbours for yachts were among the amenities offered when Queen Victoria and King Edward VII were among its distinguished visitors. The coast remains a playground, but for lesser mortals; nowadays more and more people spend their holidays in the south, but not only on the coast. Camping has made a difference. The younger and not so well off can now afford to bask in the sunshine. The French have moved in on 'development' and built themselves villas and flats for holidays and for retirement. The coast is certainly crowded, and the roads, including the coastal motorway, the *Corniche*, can be hair-raising to drive on.

You might say that, as far as foreign invasions are concerned, there had been plenty in the Midi long before the international jet-set came on the scene. The Phoeniceans established trading posts on the Mediterranean coast; the Greeks made the south of France a home from home some hundreds of years before the birth of Christ. Then the Romans came and conquered Gaul, as most of modern France was called at the time. They colonized Provence in particular, for it is certainly more like their native Italy than Britain – which they went on to conquer.

The Romans, as everyone knows, were great builders. Quite apart from leaving behind them their usual roads and fortifications, they left their architectural mark on Provence, for even today, some 2,000 years later, you can see some magnificent Roman monuments.

Even if you don't specially care about historical buildings, the Roman remains in Provence are worth looking at for their sheer size, solidity, and ability to survive through the centuries.

There was another invasion from Rome much later and it wasn't

66

Fig. 48 Roman Arena at Arles.　　Fig. 49 Le Pont du Gard.

accompanied by fighting. In 1309 the Pope, head of the Catholic Church, had to leave the Eternal City because of political pressures. He moved with his court to Avignon; the town and surrounding countryside actually became Papal property. A palace was built for him on a hill overlooking the river Rhône, and there it stands today. But the seat of the Popes moved back to Rome in 1403, and now the *Palais des Papes* can be visited and you can enjoy music festivals and other entertainments within its walls.

Fig. 50 Le Palais des Papes, Avignon.

You must have heard the famous song 'Sur le pont d'Avignon On y danse, on y danse', either in the traditional version or 'swung' by a pop group. Here is what the bridge looks like today:

Fig. 51 Avignon: le vieux pont.

Artists have also appreciated the sun, clear skies and glowing colours of Provence. At the end of the nineteenth century painters were fascinated by the light effects of the region. You are bound to have seen some re-productions of oil paintings by Cézanne and Van Gogh, for instance. You can see some of their pictures – the originals – in art galleries in London, in the Tate Gallery, the National Gallery and the Courtauld Institute. Among modern painters who have lived and painted in Provence are Matisse and Picasso, and the Englishman Graham Sutherland.

Most often reproduced pictures painted in Provence	Original can be seen in
Van Gogh	
Sunflowers	National Gallery
Cornfield with cypresses	National Gallery
Portrait of the artist with bandaged ear	Courtauld Institute
Room interior with chair with pipe	Tate Gallery – on loan from National Gallery
Cézanne	
Card Players	Courtauld Institute
View of Mont St. Victoire	Courtauld Institute

If you visit the Midi, these are some of the things you can expect to see – apart from the Roman remains:

Along the Côte d'Azur, on the coast

the blue Mediterranean Sea
some long beaches – Nice and Cannes, for instance, –
rocky coves with small beaches –
promenades with smart hotels along the sea front at resorts like Nice –
cafés and terraces with people lounging about –
people sunbathing –
people swimming –
people in boats –
people exploring under water.

Inland, in Provence

The Rhône river with small villages along its banks, and towns such as Avignon –
famous towns, e.g. Nîmes, Aix-en-Provence –
small farms –
grey-green gnarled olive trees –
vineyards –
fields of lavender where the ground is stony –
fruit trees, especially peaches –
mountains, often with rivers running in deep gorges –.

That is a selection of what you could expect to see; you could expect to feel the warm sun, but also on occasions a fierce wind called *le mistral*, which blows from the North off the Alps and seems to roar down the 'funnel' of the Rhône valley, out over the delta, or *les Bouches du Rhône*.

The flat lands of the delta have a special character. The area is called the Camargue: it used to be a watery marshland, the home of wild bulls, white horses, sea-birds and mosquitoes. Though part has been kept as a Nature Reserve, the marshes have now largely been drained and the water runs in orderly canals. Rice, sufficient to supply almost all France's needs, is now grown there. Even if there is not so much space left for the wild animals, the mosquitoes still flourish.

5. French Food and Drink

Eating

As everybody knows, French cooking is famous. For a meal to be good the ingredients have to be good too. Not necessarily expensive, but good of their kind. Care and attention have to be given to the cooking – and the eating – of a good meal, whether at home or in a restaurant. The French don't resent this. They prefer not to hurry over their food. They take it seriously and are prepared to pay for it. This applies to all types of French people. Some very good meals can be had in what in Britain would be called 'transport caffs', where you would not expect much.

Fig. 52 The sign for a good, cheap meal.

Other places where you can get simple meals or snacks are cafeterias, brasseries and bistrots. And under the influence of America and Italy, there are now any number of snack-bars and pizzerias in French towns; teenagers especially are their patrons.

It is unwise to judge French food by what you can get in Paris restaurants. In any case you have to pay more for food in large towns than in the country regions. Every region has its special dishes, which you can track down in any French cookery book.

On the whole restaurants in France don't spend so much on their interior decorations as we do in Britain. The customers behave in a more relaxed way too. Conversation is often very lively, and remarks are bandied about from table to table, possibly because restaurants have

70

FRENCH FOOD AND DRINK

CAFÉ-RESTAURANT

LA MASCOTTE

V. FROMENT

234, av. Aristide-Briand, 92 - BAGNEUX

TÉL. 253-16-37 R. C. Hauts-de-Seine 66 A 2447

MENU DU 11 - 9

Repas - a - 10ᶠ service et Boisson compris
Hors - d'œuvre
Salade de tomate
concombres en salade
saucisson beurre

Plats - du - jour

rosbif purée de pommes de terre
tranche de foie spaghetti avec tomate
côte de porc riz
merguez ou andouillette
Bifteck pommes sautées

Couvert compris		
Service	% en sus	
Serviette		

VINS DE TABLE

bout.	demie	quart
Rouge	4ᶠ50	
Blanc	6ᶠ00	
Beaujolais	14ᶠ00	
Côtes-du-Rhône	9ᶠ00	
Provence	9ᶠ00	
Bordeaux	18ᶠ00	
omelette jambon 6ᶠ00		
omelette 3 œufs 3ᶠ00		

La maison n'est pas responsable des vêtements ou objets perdus, tachés, échangés ou brûlés.

BIÈRES
1ᶠ80

EAUX MINÉRALES
4ᶠ50

Café _____ 0ᶠ80
Infusions _____ 4ᶠ50
de infusions 0ᶠ90

Apéritifs et Liqueurs de Marques

Une note détaillée sera remise au client sur sa demande.

LA NAPPE MODERNE tél. 655 46-46

Suppléments
mystère 3ᶠ00
cassate 2ᶠ50
parfait 2ᶠ50
tranche napolitaine 2ᶠ50
flan au rhum 3ᶠ00
ananas au kirsch 3ᶠ00
bavarin 3ᶠ00

a - la - carte
Hors - d'œuvre 3ᶠ00
steack au foie 10ᶠ00
chateaubriand garni 9ᶠ00
fromage ou fruit
Camembert Cantal gruyère
pont - l'évêque yaourt
pomme orange banane
poire

Fig. 53 A typical menu.

regular customers who come in every midday and/or evening for a meal. Elbows are firmly planted on the table and knives and forks waved about to emphasize a point in the argument. People don't dress up to go to a restaurant as a rule.

A table laid for a main meal may look slightly different from an English one. There won't be any side plates, so you put the hunks of the white

71

French loaves served with each course on to the table-cloth. There will probably be only one set of knife and fork per place, no matter how many courses are served. Between courses you keep your knife and fork, often resting them on your piece of bread. In a restaurant a paper 'cloth' is often laid over the woven one so that the dirty paper can be removed and a clean one put on for the next customer. The paper cloth comes in handy for working out the bill on.

You appear to be offered a large number of courses at a main meal in France. French people prefer to savour the distinctive flavour of each type of food, rather than mix it all up on one plate; they generally eat their meat, vegetables and salad separately. In actual fact you won't feel over-full at the end of the meal.

Here is a typical midday or evening meal, which varies only a little according to the habits of a particular family or the custom of a region:

MENU

Hors d'oeuvres (if mainly uncooked salads, may be called
Crudités) or
Soup   Bread
Meat   available
Vegetables (sometimes served with the meat)   on
Salad (fresh green salad with oil and vinegar dressing)   the
Cheese   table
Fresh fruit (possibly a tart or flan on Sundays)

To a certain extent it is very convenient for a French housewife to cater for her family. There is a wide choice of freshly cooked *charcuterie* readily available in the local shop even in quite small villages – ham, cooked meat, pâtés, brawn, all kinds of sausages, salads such as tomato, celery and cucumber. It means that the French eat more cold dishes than the British. When they do cook hot meals they are as likely as not to reach for the frying pan and fry a steak, for example. Hot soup at supper-time is very popular.

French housewives are still wary of frozen foods; they buy only a fifth of what is bought in Britain, but sales are increasing.

French butchers cut their meat into different joints from those the British are accustomed to, so it is sometimes quite difficult to get the right cut if you are following a recipe from a French cookery book. At the butcher's in France you can expect to pay more for lamb than for beef or pork, largely because not so much lamb is raised in France and because they have not had the benefit in the past of cheap imports from New Zealand.

72

Fig. 54 What shall we have for supper? (Bagnols-sur-Ceze, Gard.)

Special French dishes to taste if you get the chance

Soupe à l'oignon	Quenelles
Vol au vent	Coq au vin
Truites aux amandes	Boeuf bourguignon
Andouillettes	Boeuf à la mode
Tripes à la mode de Caen	Boeuf provençal

All over the Western world people are becoming weight-conscious. In France they are tending to eat less bread and to cut down on cooking with cream and butter. But wine is on the table in most families every day, and is served in works canteens and with school dinners.

Drinking

Coffee is drunk much more than tea in France, not surprisingly, because the tea is usually not much good. It is served in very small pots and you don't get a jug of hot water with it as in England. You may be offered *une tisane* – tea made of dried herbs or flowers – which is supposed to be good for, say, the nerves or the digestion. For example, *tilleul*, tea made with dried lime-flowers, may be served after the evening meal instead of coffee. The French tend to worry about their health a lot, and especially about the liver, at least judging from the number of times they refer to *le foie*. They go in for patent medicines as well as herbal remedies. And they seem to have a passion for mineral waters like Vichy or Évian, which are bottled at the source. Many French people dilute the wine they drink with their meals with plain water or *eau minérale*, which leads us to the question: what kind of wine and where is it grown?

Wine

Almost all regions of France grow grapes and make wine. On p. 75 is a map of the principal wine-growing districts.

The vineyards may be only little patches on small-holdings, or, more likely in the principal districts, stretch for mile upon mile, the vines beautifully trained and tended. Like other fruits grapes are liable to damage by frost and by disease. So there has been some progress in installing systems in some vineyards which set off heating devices automatically when the temperature falls dangerously low, as is done in some English orchards. Disease is controlled by spraying the vines with a copper sulphate solution, called 'Bordeaux mixture', which gives the leaves a blue-grey colouring. There is a lot of work to be done by hand in the vineyard.

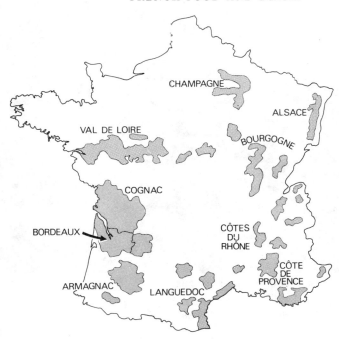

Map 11 Le vignoble français

Wine, at least *vin ordinaire*, is not a luxury in France: it is a staple crop and a necessity of life. It is usually drunk at the midday and evening meal – even for breakfast by some people – and as a pick-me-up or thirst-quencher during the day. The national production of wine in 1970 was reckoned to be in the order of 7,550 million bottles, a bottle holding about two pints. But not all this wine would actually be put into bottle; some would be distilled into spirits, some drunk straight from the cask, and the surplus distilled for industrial alcohol. Small wonder, nevertheless, that France has a problem of alcoholism.

But there are wines and wines, some stronger, some more choice, some 'young', some more mature. The quality varies between regions, and also between vineyards in the same village. You sometimes hear the expression 'vintage wine'. This means that the exact origin of the wine is stated. Vintage wine – *un grand vin* or *un vin de marque* – is of high quality, and as expensive in France as when exported. The word 'vintage' on its own can mean the crop, or the gathering of the grapes to make wine.

75

Fig. 55 Vineyard at Château d'Yquem, Bordeaux.

Different categories of French wines

Vins ordinaires to be drunk every day, cheap enough for anybody, sometimes called 'plonk' in English slang. These wines may be blended, i.e. they may consist of a mixture of different qualities from different places; or they may be local wines, *vins du pays*.

Vins de qualité supérieure These are better wines and the bottles bear the label V.D.Q.S.

Vins d'appellation contrôlée guaranteed vintage wines which by government regulation are made only from certain types of grapes in certain specific areas, and are of a guaranteed strength.

Domaine and château wines produced and bottled on a particular estate and famous throughout the world.

The main wine-producing areas of France

Bordeaux Some of the most famous parts of this area are called Médoc, Saint Émilion, Grave, and Sauternes, and the wines take their general name from them; for example, one says, 'This is a Sauternes.' Also, in the Bordeaux area a wine from a particular estate is automatically called a 'château wine'; there are about 1,500 'châteaux'. In England red wine from Bordeaux is often called 'claret' because it is a clear light red colour.

Burgundy	Wines of high quality come from this area. Districts which give their name to wines include Côte de Nuits, Côte de Beaune, Chablis, Mâcon and Beaujolais. The reds are heavier, and have more 'body' than the Bordeaux clarets.
Côtes du Rhone and Provence	Good wines are produced here, but they are less famous.
Champagne	This area produces the sparkling wine especially famous in England for being drunk at weddings; called 'bubbly' because it is fizzy.
Charentes	Cognac, i.e. brandy, is named after the town in this area. It is a spirit distilled from wine.

The wine-bottle label test

Cheapest	Label shows trade-mark but no other details. Wine is a mixture from various regions, possibly also from Algeria, North Africa.
Not so Cheap	Label shows name of an area, e.g. Bourgogne, Loire. Wine is a mixture of wines from that area.
Dearer	Label shows name of precise part of an area, e.g. Sauternes, Beaune. Wine has some distinction and character, taste or smell, i.e. a 'bouquet'.
Dearest	Label shows name of a particular plot of land – 'le clos' in Burgundy, 'le château' in Bordeaux area – or sometimes shows just the owner's name, e.g. Rothschild. It also shows the year the wine was made, i.e. its vintage. This kind of wine is very special and fetches high prices. The year it was grown matters; some years are better than others.

The larger the area mentioned on the label, the cheaper the wine.

One area of the south of France, the Languedoc, produces 12 per cent of all the wine in the world and 40 per cent of French wine. But 81 per cent of wine from Languedoc is *vin ordinaire*, of the kind that French people drink every day. That is why its name is not so well known abroad. On the whole only the better wines are exported, though the rising price of wine and increasing wine-consumption by countries like Britain may lead to more *ordinaire* being sold abroad.

6. Getting Equipped to Earn a Living

The education system

French schools are, in the main, State schools. *L'enseignement public* refers to the whole State system, including the universities. There are some private schools called *écoles privés* or *écoles libres*. Many of these are run by the Catholic Church, and in some there is a Protestant influence. About 10 % of French children are educated privately. In recent years some private schools have been given grants by the State, and are now run under the same rules and regulations. But there are a number of people who resent this money being granted because they are against the Church and clergy – a feeling that is traditional in some sections of French society.

Total no. of pupils in 1971–72 *in*	
State schools	9,925,981
Private schools	1,940,513

The big difference between State and private schools is that by a law passed in 1882 no religious education of any kind may be given in State schools. Otherwise the difference is becoming less obvious. The Church in France is modernizing itself, and that is being felt in its schools. On the other hand the State schools have realized since May 1968 that they are more in danger of a take-over by political theorists, i.e. Marxists, than by religious teachers looking for converts.

How the schools are run

It is no surprise to find that the school system is run from a Ministry in Paris. So are most other departments of French public life.

There are no Local Education Authorities in France. The local administrator is called *le recteur de l'académie*. He controls all the educational establishments in his area as a representative of the Ministry of Education.

All schools of the same type in France are run exactly according to the same pattern. Every year the Ministry of Education publishes a handbook. It contains information and also regulations controlling in the minutest detail the organization of each type of school and the work that staff and students will perform. There is complete centralization, apart from an innovation made in 1973 when 10 per cent of lesson time was 'freed' by the

Ministry, enabling the schools to arrange some of their own activities.
Examples of what the Ministry controls in every school:

1. The subjects to be taught.
2. The number of lessons per week to be given to each subject.
3. The detailed syllabus of the work to be covered in each subject during the three school terms of each year, in every age-group, in each particular type of school, and in every option.
4. The actual textbooks to be used in class (there may be a choice from a limited range).
5. The detailed syllabus of all examinations – entrance exams, leaving-certificate exams, internal exams on which a pupil's promotion depends.

What this system means is that, depending on your age and type of school, you will be having the same education wherever you live in France. Say you are a twelve-year-old in a school in the south of France. You will be taking the same subjects, be covering the same syllabus and use more or less the same books, at the same time as your counterpart in any other region of France.

The Ministry in Paris decides what kind of schools and how many shall be built – and where. A rural area sometimes comes off badly compared with a densely populated urban area because the Ministry doesn't allow it an adequate variety of schools.

'L'enseignement public est gratuit'

True. Education is free right through to the end of the primary school. But in secondary schools, for the 11 – 15-year-olds in Cycle 1, parents have to contribute something towards their children's education because the money provided by the State is not enough.

There are grants and bursaries for clever pupils and for the very poor, but the French complain that they are insufficient.

Changes in the system

In May 1968 a revolution swept through the universities. The students demanded changes in the system and wanted a say in how they were taught. The revolution spread to the top classes of the secondary schools, where in some cases the older pupils took over and occupied their school. It really shook things up. So there has been a reorganization of the school system, but it is not completed yet. Some people feel it never will be, and some that the changes are more in name than reality.

Under the old system you had to take an exam at 11 which separated the sheep from the goats. The privileged 'sheep' went on to the secondary schools, the rest stayed on in *le Primaire* until they reached school-leaving age.

Under the new system there is a kind of committee which decides after referring to your primary-school record to which of three types of secondary school you will go.

Here is a chart of the new school system:

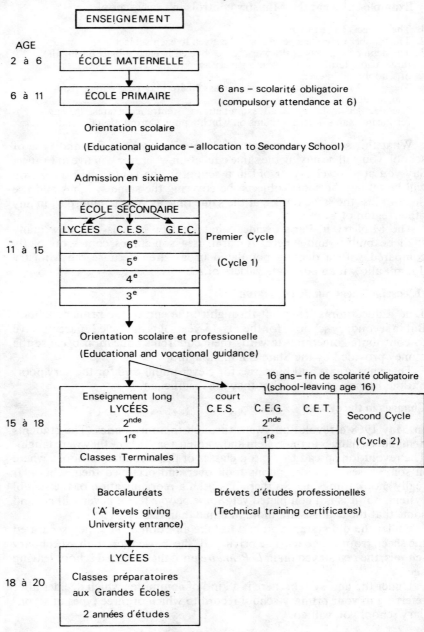

ENSEIGNEMENT

AGE

2 à 6   ÉCOLE MATERNELLE

6 à 11   ÉCOLE PRIMAIRE   6 ans – scolarité obligatoire
                                              (compulsory attendance at 6)

Orientation scolaire

(Educational guidance – allocation to Secondary School)

Admission en sixième

ÉCOLE SECONDAIRE

LYCÉES   C.E.S.   G.E.C.   Premier Cycle

11 à 15 6e (Cycle 1)

                  5^e

                  4^e

                  3^e

Orientation scolaire et professionelle

(Educational and vocational guidance)

                                    16 ans – fin de scolarité obligatoire
                                    (school-leaving age 16)

Enseignement long   court
LYCÉES   C.E.S.   C.E.G.   C.E.T.   Second Cycle

15 à 18 2nde 2nde

           1re 1re (Cycle 2)

Classes Terminales

Baccalauréats   Brévets d'études professionelles

('A' levels giving   (Technical training certificates)
University entrance)

LYCÉES

Classes préparatoires

18 à 20   aux Grandes Écoles

2 années d'études

A Guide to the School System (dating from 1968)

L' École Maternelle 2 – 6
Nursery + Infant School. There are not enough of these. More places are
promised for the 4- and 5-year-olds.

L' École Primaire 6 – 11   Middle Infants to Top Junior classes
Timetable for the week
French – 10 hours
Maths –   5 hours
'Stimulating Activities' – 6 hours
include history, geography, moral education, art, craft, music, and
everything else *except*
Physical education – 6 hours
but this is unlikely in fact to be as much because of lack of staff,
facilities, and equipment.

Orientation Scolaire
Guidance given by a 'Commission d'admission'
to each pupil about transfer to a particular type of
secondary school. Committee appointed by the local
school administrator.
Advice given based on Primary school reports and parents' wishes.

Admission en sixième
French secondary schools begin with the Sixth Form at 11.
You reach the First Form at about 17 if you stay on beyond the
school-leaving age of 16. You can complete your school studies
in a 'Classe Terminale'.

L' École Secondaire
Secondary education is divided into two cycles.
Cycle 1 = 4 years from Class 6 to Class 3
Cycle 2 (long) = 3 years
Cycle 2 (short) = 2 years
depending on which school-leaving exam you take.

At the Orientation Scolaire you will have been
guided – or just transferred – to one of three
kinds of secondary school. They are supposed to
offer equal opportunities. Nobody knows whether
they ever will.

Orientation scolaire et professionelle

Educational and vocational guidance: an important hurdle to be got over,
even though an exam is not necessarily involved. A 'Conseil d'orientation',
a council, advises individual pupils and their parents about career prospects,
school courses in Cycle 2, and other training courses.
The council includes the Head of the Upper School running Cycle 2, an
inspector of technical education, and representative parents. If you don't
accept its advice, you have to take a qualifying exam for the course of your
choice.

Fin de scolarité obligatoire

School-leaving age = 16
If you leave school at 16 there are apprenticeship and other training schemes (see p. 91)

Enseignement long

Three-year courses in Cycle 2 (leading to the Baccalauréat; see below) which have a number of main subjects plus options to choose from. The choices are increasing and changing, but whatever you choose you always have to continue in both Arts and Science subjects, all of which are examinable.
New three-year technical courses have been introduced – enseignements des sciences et des techniques industrielles fondamentales. 'Enseignement long' runs in lycées. The technical courses also run in special lycées techniques.

Enseignement court

Two-year courses in Cycle 2 (leading to Brevets d'études professionelles), which combine general education with vocational training; also run in the C.E.T.s (Collèges d'Enseignement Technique; see p. 83).

Le Baccalauréat

Commonly known as le bac.
Written and oral exam taken at the end of a three-year course.
Gives entry to university.
Consists of long essays on (1) general subjects, and (2) special subjects, arranged under broad headings. Here are some examples:
  Philo et Lettres (Philosophy and Literature)
  Économique et Social
  Économique
  Mathématiques et Sciences Physiques
  Mathématiques et Sciences Natures
  Sciences agronomiques et techniques
  Informatique
  Mathématiques et Technique
  Sciences médico-sociales
  Musique

The failure rate in the bac in 1975 was 33 per cent.

After the *bac* the brightest students can stay on for two years in some of the big lycées, which have 'classes préparatoires' for the fearsomely competitive entrance exam to the 'Grandes Ecoles' (see p. 89 on Higher Education). It means that some schools will have 18–20-year-olds within their walls, strengthening the impression that French schoolchildren look more and more grown-up these days. The competitive exam makes the 'classes préparatoires' work very hard indeed. French pupils of all ages seem to stick hard at their school work. Don't imagine that they are impelled by a love of learning; it just seems to be part of school life.

Fig. 56 Lycée Polyvalent de Bellegarde.

Lycées

The 'Grammar' Schools: 18.4 per cent of all secondary schools. Relatively unchanged; specialize in Cycle 2 courses.

CES   Collèges d'enseignement secondaire

Comprehensive Schools(?)
Either a new school or a refurbished former CEG (see below), or an almost independent section within a large lycée (see above).
They have had difficulty in becoming established and accepted.

CET   Collèges d'enseignement technique

Technical secondary schools, sometimes an annexe to a lycée, offering two-year technical and practical courses to students from age 15 onwards.

CEG   Collèges d'enseignement général

Secondary — or former Secondary Modern — schools.
To be found especially in country regions; they provide a basic education for Cycle 1. There are specialist teachers on the staff. These schools may disappear eventually.

School life

French schools are geared to giving each child a sound knowledge of French literature, history, and what we call 'culture', as well as a thorough training of the mind. What this aim amounts to is to teach the child about his French heritage from the past and to limber up his thinking so that he can argue logically and discuss fluently. Note that there is so far little mention of 'discovery methods' or of stimulating the creative imagination.

School work at all age-levels involves a great deal of learning by heart, and of essay-writing on rather abstract subjects.

The teacher's job is to help the pupils to make progress with their school work by giving them information, supervising their work, and testing it. In France the teacher is not required to look after his pupils' general welfare: he doesn't get the opportunity, in any case, since he only sees them during lesson time. You can guess that the French educational system is not directed towards letting the personality of the young develop, or even concerned with producing good citizens or leaders of the community. It is accepted by staff and pupils that school is a place you come to do a job of work in impersonal, inflexible surroundings. What the pupils do outside school hours is nothing to do with the school.

When the revolution of May 1968 spread to the schools, students formed committees to discuss what was wrong with the educational system and how to change it. They argued day and night, and many teachers joined in. Detailed proposals for reform were produced.

The Minister for Education promised to act, and there have been some changes in school organization, in what is taught, and how it is taught. In 1972 some schools were chosen as experimental schools, to act as guinea-pigs in research on possible changes. Reform is in the air, but on the whole life in school goes on much as it ever did.

Daily Timetable

---

8 a.m. School *begins*, generally.
No assembly at any time.
Length of *each lesson* = 1 hour.
Midday break between 12 noon and 1 o'clock.
School dinner for many pupils.
Two or three *lessons* in the *afternoon*.
Afterwards '*études*' – supervised homework sessions – for those whose parents want them to stay at school.

Wednesday is a whole day off: it used to be Thursdays.
Saturday morning: school is in session.

School work

There is no streaming or setting; you stay with your class for all subjects. If you don't make the grade at the end of the school year, you stay down. This could happen several times which worries both parents and the educational authorities. The number in a class varies from 18 to 45, the average being 34.

Lessons usually follow the pattern:
(a) testing facts given in the last lesson;
(b) expounding of new material by the teacher;
(c) assigning of homework.

There is not usually any discussion involving the class or a pupil's opinions.

There is no homework timetable. Each teacher sets what he or she thinks fit. It may take the pupil all the evening to do.

Written and oral work is marked out of 10 or 20; for example, *3 sur 10, 12 sur 20*.

Discipline

A teacher's responsibility for order is confined to his own classroom during his own lessons.

Any serious misconduct can be reported *not* to the Head Teacher but to the *conseiller d'éducation*, who is in charge of the *surveillants*.

A *surveillant(e)* keeps order in the school everywhere except in the classroom during lessons – rather like an usher in nineteenth-century British schools. He or she is usually a student who needs the money to finish studies or training.

The job of a *surveillant* in a French school is by no means easy. French children, repressed by the formality in class, tend to break out at mealtimes and in the playground, to compensate.

Some schools have tried to get the senior pupils to take some responsibility for school discipline by having an elected school council of seniors, but although some strong leaders emerged during the 'events' of May 1968, councils of monitors or prefects have not been a success. The old French individualist spirit rises up and refuses to be subordinated to someone else of equal rank. Not only children but their parents, too, protested.

Games and physical education

School team-games may help to develop a community spirit, but they don't play a large part in school life, and you don't often see extensive playing-fields attached to or for the exclusive use of schools in France. Because of lack of gymnasia and equipment the number of gym lessons in reality is smaller than that specified on the timetable. More specialist trained teachers are needed. The Ministry is trying to improve the situation, but it takes time and money.

Time allotted to P.E. by Ministry regulation		
Primary School	age 6–11	6 hours
Secondary School –		
Cycle 1	age 11–15	3 hours
Cycle 2	age 15–18	2 hours

In fact schools overcome the lack of sports facilities by using community sports centre or *Centres d'animation sportive*. Priority is given to schoolchildren, and entrance is free in term-time and holidays alike. The aim was to open 300 more such sports centres during 1973.

A special feature of French school life is the departure during term-time of whole classes – in winter and summer alike – to take up residence in hotels and hostels for up to four weeks in the mountains, or by the sea, or in the country. These 'school journeys' are called *Classes de neige, Classes de mer, Classes vertes.*

Fig. 57 *Enfants de Cachan en classe de neige à la Chapelle d'Abondance.*

Members of staff accompany the classes and lessons take place in the morning. In the afternoon the class goes out and you can learn or improve your skiing or swimming or whatever. As many as 60,000 children a year go to the mountains with their school-mates.

School holidays.

The dates are fixed by the Ministry in Paris, though they may vary slightly from area to area.

VIVE
LA
RENTRÉE

Fig. 58

School Holidays 1974–75

---

113 days in the year
Three areas: Zone B   Paris
                Zone C   Poitiers, Limoges, Rheims, Dijon, Strasbourg, Besançon, Grenoble, Montpelier
                Zone A   The rest of the country

For All Saints:	from Tuesday 29 October after school to Monday a.m., 4 November 1974.
For Christmas:	from Saturday 21 December after school to Friday a.m., 3 January 1975
In February:	Zone A, from Saturday 1 February to Monday 10 February.
	Zone B, from Saturday 8 February to Monday 17 February.
	Zone C, from Saturday 15 February to Monday 24 February.
For Easter:	Saturday 22 March to Monday 7 April.
Summer Holidays:	Saturday 28 June to Monday 15 September. –
Back to school:	all on the same day, early in September.

Higher education

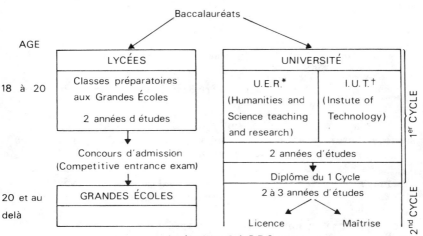

LES ENSEIGNEMENTS SUPÉRIEURS

Baccalauréats

AGE

	LYCÉES	UNIVERSITÉ	
18 à 20	Classes préparatoires aux Grandes Écoles 2 années d études	U.E.R.* (Humanities and Science teaching and research)	I.U.T.† (Instute of Technology)

1ᵉʳ CYCLE

Concours d'admission (Competitive entrance exam)

2 années d'études
Diplôme du 1 Cycle

20 et au delà	GRANDES ÉCOLES	2 à 3 années d'études

Licence   Maîtrise

2ⁿᵈ CYCLE

Agrégations, C.A.P.E.S. etc.

*U.E.R.: Unités d'études et de recherches
† I.U.T.: Institut universitaire de technologie

Some of the exams and when you take them

At the end of two years	DUEL *Diplôme universitaire d'études littéraires* DUES *Diplôme universitaire d'études scientifiques*
at the end of three years	LICENCE First University Degree
at the end of four years	CAPES *Certificat d'Aptitude au Professorat de l'Enseignement Secondaire* (Graduate certificate for teaching in secondary schools – competitive)
at the end of five years	MAÎTRISE Second University Degree – Master of Arts or of Science
Then you can take the	AGRÉGATION, a very competitive exam with high status.

Finally you may take the DOCTORAT, a research degree, after possibly fifteen years' work.

From 1975, at the end of the first two years a new exam will be taken: DEUG (*Diplôme d'études universitaires générales*), for all faculties except pharmacology and dentistry. It will be based on a more general syllabus.

The student riots of May 1968 led to changes in the law governing French higher education. Now changes are being attempted from within the universities themselves, regrouping the subjects to be studied so that you can take a course in more than one area of knowledge.

But the chief characteristics of the universities remain the same:

You can enter a university if you have the *bac*. All you have to do is to register at the admissions office.

There are no interviews.

There is no limit to the number of students except in the medical sciences.

This may sound splendid, but there are drawbacks once you are a student: there is no one to guide you, no personal tutor, no seminar groups with a tutor. You won't have any personal contact with members of staff.

There are lectures to attend in huge overcrowded halls. If you arrive late, you may have to sit in the corridor outside. At the end of the year you take an exam. The results determine whether you go on to the next stage of your studies.

You may be very lonely because there are not many students' clubs and not enough halls of residence (*foyers*).

Being a student is expensive. True, tuition fees are low, but everything else, books, living in a city, and so on, is very dear. There are hardly any grants available.

The 'Grandes Écoles'

These establishments are very special. They are independent of the universities and come under the authority of various ministries for whom, to a certain extent, they are producing highly trained professional men.

The 'Grandes Écoles' cream off the best brains and give their owners a privileged education and training – usually residential and free – which leads its brilliant and tenacious graduates straight to the top in public life, in the arts, or in scientific research.

Three of the most famous 'Grandes Écoles'

L'École Polytechnique Founded in 1795 to train engineers and professional men for government service and the Army. Still commanded by a general. Graduates now go on to work in private enterprise and the civil service as well as the armed forces.
Famous ex-student – Giscard d'Estaing.

L'École Normale Supérieure

Very high level of scholarship in the humanities and sciences. Unstuffy atmosphere. Famous ex-students: Sartre, Pompidou.

L'École Nationale d'Administration

Founded in 1946. Postgraduate institution specializing in politics, economics, sociology. Held in high esteem in the Civil Service.

The French are not particularly prone to gang up or form clubs, but the ex-students of the 'Grandes Écoles' tend to form an old-boy network in the places of power throughout France – which is unusual and comes in for some criticism. There is no doubt that men gain prestige from having been students at a Grande École, and this rubs off on their jobs. For example, Polytechnician engineers and technocrats have raised the standing of engineering and technology in the eyes of French people, especially since 1945, and helped France to enjoy economic prosperity. French education has always had a reputation for being highly selective, and the *lycées* and *Grandes Écoles* have been noted as 'hot-houses' breeding an élite. In spite of attempts to modernize the system and broaden the curriculum, selection is still a fact of French life. The educational system has been called *une véritable machine à selection par l'échec*, 'check' as in chess, or 'failure'.

89

Fig. 59 *Le 'recyclage' des parents*. The nightmare of modern maths.

Continuing Education and Retraining

A second, and even a third, chance to educate yourself later in life or to be retrained in a new skill is being very much boosted in France. A law was passed in 1971 providing among other things for someone who has been in a job for three years to have up to a year off to go on a training course to up-date his skills or learn new ones – a process called *recyclage*. The French speak of *la formation permanente*, meaning that you need never cease to go on learning throughout your life. Figure 59 shows parents facing up to *'le cauchemar des maths modernes'*.

Training for a job

On leaving school

All over the world there is less and less work for unskilled people and a general demand for skilled workers; France is no exception. So training opportunities for the young in France are very important for their future – though that is not to say that all school-leavers bother about training.

But of course some people never seem to have any problems about deciding what they want to do or to be when they leave school. The brightest ones often stay on until they have taken the exams which admit them to a university; in France that means the *bac*. With their *bac* they can get on with their education and training to become doctors, dentists, civil servants, engineers, and other professional people.

What happens to young people in France who have not got a definite vocation or who aren't necessarily academically inclined is not so clear-cut. And there are some whose parents can't afford to pay for a lengthy professional training; the grants which you get automatically in Britain if you are accepted by a university or college are not given so liberally in other countries – and certainly not in France.

In France the school-leaving age is 16, so when you are 16 you can legally walk out and look for a job. But in France, as in Britain, you are unlikely to find anything worth while just like that. As in Britain, if a boy wants to be a skilled mechanic or an engineer in a factory, he can become an apprentice, 'bound' under contract to an employer, learning the skills by working alongside fully trained professionals in the workshop. For a girl there are fewer opportunities.

In 1971 a law was passed by the French parliament which reduced the number of years an apprentice had to serve from three to two. It laid down that he was to be released from work to study the skills of his craft for ten hours a week. It also said that an apprentice is to be treated the same as a fully qualified worker and receive a guaranteed minimum wage.

The wage-rates for apprentices in French industry are being regulated from now on, so that at the outset they will get 15 per cent of the national guaranteed minimum wage, rising to 45 per cent at the end of their apprenticeship.

The French apprentice spends his ten hours a week of day-release training either in technical classes run by some large employers, or, if they don't exist, he goes to a college called a *Collège d'Enseignment Technique*, or *C.E.T*. There are over half a million students at these 'techs' in France.

Suppose you can't get an apprenticeship, or you want to train for some job which doesn't have an apprenticeship scheme; in such a case a French boy or girl can transfer from the secondary school before the age of 15 and go full-time to a *C.E.T.*. One-third of the secondary-school population does so.

The French set great store by examinations. At the *C.E.T*.s French students will be working towards some kind of certificate or diploma. This will be their entrance 'ticket' to a job. A one-year course will lead to a *Certificat d'Éducation Professionelle* or *C.E.P.*, a three-year course to a *Certificat d'Aptitude Professionelle* or *C.A.P.*

But there is a lot of criticism of the *C.E.T*.s in France. The number of students in practical classes is often too big, so that there is not enough apparatus to go round. The teaching at some *C.E.T*.s has been called *un enseignment pauvre pour les pauvres*. You may get pushed on to a particular course just because there is room. If your parents have money, you can go to a private school or college and get your training there. Or you might take a correspondence course. You can still take the exams and get the all-important certificate.

Fig. 60 A class hard at work in a lycée technique.

If you were doing really well at school you might be able to aim at higher technical qualifications by entering a *Lycée Technique* or Technical High School at 15. You could follow a three-year specialized course, for example in catering, in heating and ventilation engineering, or to be a fitter, or an electronics technician, or an animal technician in a laboratory, or a theatre technician in a hospital. Success in the examination will bring you either a *bac* in technical subjects or a diploma, a *Brevet de Technicien*. There are a quarter of a million students at the *Lycées Techniques*.

Of course, a few boys and girls take a longer training in technology at the very highest level and obtain the highest qualifications – degrees – at a technological university, *un Institut Universitaire de Technologie* or *I.U.T*. Only about 27,000 students attend these institutes.

Whatever the level aimed at, it is important to get some kind of qualification in France so that, when you go looking for a job, you have a piece of paper to flourish at your prospective employer.

Where to live while training

Suppose a French boy or girl living in the provinces decides that there's no future for him there and goes off to Paris to learn a trade; the biggest problem might very well be, where to live in the big city. A residential club or hostel might be the answer – a *Foyer de Jeunes Travailleurs* – catering for someone either in a steady job or on a training course. There were 60,000 young people placed in clubs in 1973, and in the Paris region 13,000 beds are available. There is also a lodgings bureau, *le Centre du logement des apprentis et jeunes travailleurs*, which has reasonably priced private accommodation on offer – only there is never enough of it.

In English the word 'hostel' puts many people off. They would not consider living in one. In French the word *foyer* means fireside, hearth, or centre, and the *Foyers de Jeunes Travailleurs* are places where young people can find entertainment and meals too, as well as a roof over their heads. The size of the *foyer* varies from the homely ones for about thirty teenagers, aged about 16 to 20, to the large ones for upwards of 150 rather older young workers, from about 18 to 25. The larger ones are more like hotels.

One thing all the *foyers* have in common: they have an older person in charge and they offer all kinds of educational and cultural activities as well as television, a library, a discothèque, sports facilities, and studios where you can paint or do pottery. They also provide rooms where the residents can work quietly, because many of them will be studying part-time or full-time to get better qualifications. Some of the residential clubs have an *animateur* on the staff whose job it is to keep community life going, to introduce new activities, and generally liven things up. More and more clubs are being opened so that there are now over 6,000 people professionally involved in running hostels; courses are being laid on to train more staff.

Quite apart from having to see to the cleaning and housekeeping of the clubs, the staff is closely involved with the welfare of the residents. The idea is that the director or his assistants should be available at all times to help the young residents if need be, and to overcome the sense of isolation which you can easily feel if you are a stranger in a big city.

The restaurant of a *foyer* can be a good place to overcome shyness and isolation. Many restaurants are open to non-residents; they must be good because some serve five and six times more meals than there are residents in the club. Prices are reasonable because the young apprentice or worker doesn't have much money. You can share a room with one or two others and get half-board for 340 to 350 francs per month (under £9 per week at 1973 prices).

All these provisions are paid for partly from the young worker's earnings, partly by subsidies out of local and government taxes to the *foyer*, and partly by grants to individual residents from government agencies like the Ministry of Social Security. Obviously the *foyers* fulfil a need. They seem to be popular with young people, for they are mostly not attached to any factories, firms or trades but are apparently without strings. The *foyers* have formed themselves into a federation – *Union des Foyers de Jeunes Travailleurs* – which supplies information about improvements in and expansion of the service to young people in training or working for a living.

National Service

Conscription to the armed forces or community services is something that Britain has only experienced in time of war and the immediate post-war years. National Service ended in the UK in 1960. In France it has

Fig. 61 Soldiers go off on leave.

been a feature of young men's lives since 1905. It still operates today.

Under a law passed in 1970 and amended in 1973, a French male citizen is liable for National Service at the age of 20, but if it suits him better he can choose to be called up at 18, given the agreement of his parents or guardians. He can also ask for his call-up to be deferred till he is 22. He has to serve for one year.

Young men who are training to be doctors or vets can have their call-up deferred until they are 27, dentists and pharmacists until 25. They are likely to be posted then to units in the armed services where they can practise on the troops.

If you have had at least one year's higher education and want to use your special skills during your national service, you can apply for deferment till you are 25. You may be able, for example, to work in a technical aid programme provided by the army to an underdeveloped country overseas.

But there is a snag in asking for such special treatment. In all cases you have to serve four months extra. But it is usually worth it because you can complete your education or training without interruption before doing your national service, and you also have a better chance of promotion while you are serving.

In some ways girls in France are lucky. National service is not compulsory for them, but since May 1972, as an experiment they are allowed to volunteer for a year if they are unmarried, or widows with no dependent children, and if they are between 18 and 27 years old. They can serve as interpreters, translators, drivers, or clerks.

94

7. Working Life in France

The pattern of working life has been changing during the last 25 years.

1973 Total French working population = 21.5 million

1974 Total French working population = 21.1 million

Agricultural workers as a percentage of the total French work force

1958	20%
1971	13%
1973	10%

In 1973 there were just over 2 million people working on the land. The number continues to fall. When agricultural workers leave the farms they often go into factories and workshops. So then they count as industrial workers.

In 1973 the number of people employed in industry, building and civil engineering was 8 million. Over 10 million had jobs in transport, trade, administration and all kinds of services – 50 per cent of the working population.

Conditions of work

No matter in what country you work, you tend to have the same worries:

how much money is there in my pay packet?
how long is the working week?
how long are my holidays?

By law a French worker has the right to

a 40-hour week + overtime,
4 weeks or 24 working days' holiday with pay per year,
6 to 8 days public holidays, some unpaid, per year.

Here are the public 'Bank holidays' in France:

le lundi de Pâques	Easter Monday
le 1er mai	Labour Day (paid holiday)
le 14 juillet	Fête Nationale (celebration of the storming of the Bastille prison during the French Revolution in 1789).
le 15 août	Assumption of the Virgin Mary

95

la Toussaint	All Saints' Day, 1st November.
le 11 novembre	commemorating the end of World War I.
Noël	Christmas Day
le Nouvel An	New Year's Day

The industrial worker

It is difficult to indicate how much money French workers get in their pay packets, because rates of pay are bound to alter and the rate of exchange between the French franc and other currencies alters too. But the spread of incomes as between various types of French workers can be seen in a diagram:

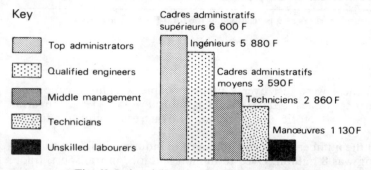

Fig. 62 Industrial workers' monthly salaries for July 1973

There are some general points to be made about wages and salaries in France.

1. There is a guaranteed minimum wage – *un salaire minimum interprofessionel garanti*, otherwise known as *SMIG*; now replaced by *SMIC*, in which the C stands for *de croissance* (increasing, rising, to allow for inflation).
2. Hourly wage rates are on the way out and are being replaced by monthly salary payments – *un salaire payé au mois*.

A guaranteed minimum wage ensures that nobody's wages fall below a certain fixed level. Monthly salary payments are sought after because they raise the status of manual workers to that of white-collar workers like office staff. Also, there is more job security for a salaried worker; you are not so liable to instant dismissal. There is more money in it, too; and if you are changing over from weekly to monthly payments, you may be able to get an advance to tide you over to the end of the first month or so.

Trade unions in France

In an industrial society the workers organize themselves into trade unions in order to protect their interests – their wages, their standard of living, the conditions in which they work. In Britain you generally join the particular union concerned with your kind of work, craft or profession. French trade unions are called *syndicats*.

There are several different unions competing for the membership of the same kind of workers.

The biggest and best known union is the C.G.T. – *Confédération Générale du Travail*.

In Britain the unions are closely associated with the Labour Party; in France, apart from the Communist C.G.T., they claim to be independent of all left-wing political parties. It is traditional in France for the unions to distrust *all* political involvement.

In France the number of trade-union members is smaller than in other major industrial countries.

There is no equivalent of the Trades Union Congress (T.U.C.) in France, because of the rivalry between the unions.

Percentage of working population
who are members of a Trade Union

Britain	45%
France	20%

Workers' participation

Since World War II workers in French factories have been increasingly involved in making decisions about the running of their factory, and in sharing the profits.

Delegates are elected from the shop floor, and recognized trade unions put up candidates for election to works committees, which guide the policy and working of the factory.

Since 1967 it has been compulsory in French factories employing more than 100 workers for them to share the profits. The share may not be higher than 3 per cent of any individual's wage packet. The amount and method of payment of the share has to be worked out by employer and employed together. The unions are not all in favour of profit-sharing because some of them believe it puts the workers in the same class as the employers and weakens their wish to alter the way things are organized.

The agricultural worker

You need to keep reminding yourself that there is a lot of agricultural land in France, and that there are still many small farms. The plots of land farmed by one man are often scattered as the result of a law which in the old days made sure that, when parents died, their property was divided equally among all their children. Each one got a piece of plough-land, of grazing land, of forest, whatever happened to be in the inheritance.

The result is a patchwork pattern most unsuitable for working with modern farm machinery.

So farmers went on using old-fashioned methods, growing a bit of this and a bit of that, producing enough to feed their own families and selling the small surplus at the local market – a hen, some eggs, and a few pounds of butter perhaps. The farmer thought this was a safe kind of life, especially in war-time when food was short. At least his own family didn't have to suffer.

In the end the young farmers of France began to revolt against their parents' stick-in-the-mud attitudes. They started to form co-operatives to buy machinery and plots of land to use in common. They started demonstrations to put pressure on the government to help them to modernize. One of their banners read: *L'Agriculture de Papa est morte.*

The government took notice. It encourages villagers to swap small 'parcels' of land in order to piece together larger units, and offers help with the cost of digging out hedges, filling in ditches, and drainage. They call the whole operation *le remembrement*, and it is certainly beginning to change the look of some parts of rural France.

Fig. 63 *Remembrement:* before.   Fig. 64 *Remembrement:* after.

By 1972, 200,000 elderly farmers had been encouraged by government pay-outs to leave their holdings. Young farmers have been helped to settle in reorganized farming areas.

People earning their living from the land are getting a better deal nowadays in France because they can sell their produce more easily and regularly; for example, to new canning factories, to co-operatives making butter and cheese, and to others making wine. It looks as though fewer workers on the land are going to produce more and better-quality crops, earn more for themselves, and even improve their conditions of work sufficiently to be able to take a holiday now and again.

Modernizing French agriculture is not a simple or speedy matter, however. In order to keep the many remaining peasant farmers moderately satisfied and calm the fears of those who want the countryside to go on looking the way it has for centuries, subsidies have to be given, and high prices paid for food. Overproduction can result. In some ways it is a wasteful process, as the government realizes; and it is certainly often resented by town-dwellers when they go shopping. But the very same shoppers have a sentimental attachment to rural France. They feel they come from there, forgetting how many generations ago that may be.

Half the farmers of Europe are French

A third of the farm-land of the nine countries of the EEC is French

Small wonder that the French have a special interest in the policy of the European Common Market for agriculture, and in the prices and quantities of farm produce that are agreed by the Commission.

The rest of the working population

A third group of workers, distinct from the agricultural and industrial workers, do not have much in common with one another, but they are all non-productive. They work, for example, in the 'service' industries and they form the largest – and still growing – section of the working population. Their numbers do not include housewives and students, who, apparently, are not reckoned to *work*.

Many of the third group of workers are involved in marketing the products of the first two groups, who work in agriculture and industry. The third group earn their living in commerce, or as installers or repairers of technical goods, or as shop assistants or in the distributive trades.

In France as in other Western countries the small shopkeeper who runs a family business is steadily disappearing. Like the owners of small unprofitable farms, he clings to his business in spite of the threat from the growing number of self-service shops, even in small out-of-the-way towns. It seems that there are still enough customers, especially among the elderly and lonely, who prefer to shop where they can have a chat with the proprietor, not about the weather as in England, but about their state of health, their neighbours, their family, the corruption of the government of the day, the misdeeds of 'them', whoever they may be. The shopkeeper accumulates a good deal of information about his customers' families and learns to ask the right questions.

99

Victory over the modernizers?

1. In October 1973 a Bill concerning the future development of commerce was before the French National Assembly.

2. In the Bill local commissions were to decide what new retail shops are to be given planning permission to open.

3. The question was whether local small shopkeepers sitting on the commission were to have half the seats – with local councillors and local consumers occupying the other half.

4. Result – a national campaign including 'sit-ins' in 100 Chambers of Commerce by small shopkeepers to get a Bill passed to give them at least half the seats.

5. The Bill was passed by 295 votes to 0.

6. How many new supermarkets are going to get planning permission to open in future?

As long as there are a few old people's clubs or community centres the small shop fulfils a social function. If the small shop disappears the appearance of a French street, in town or village alike, will change.

Here are some typical shops which might get swallowed up behind the plate-glass windows of supermarkets:

la boucherie	The butcher's, where you can buy any cut of meat except pork.
la charcuterie	Pork meat is sold here, and pork products include ham, sausages, slices of various sausages; also pâtés and salads. Just the kind of place to shop at for picnics if you are a tourist.
la boulangerie	The baker bakes twice a day. At his shop you buy the typical French loaf, *une baguette*, long and thin; also crescent-shaped *croissants* and bun-shaped *brioches* to eat for breakfast.
l'épicerie	At the grocer's the usual dry goods like sugar are on sale, and probably also fruit, vegetables, cheese, ham – and wine for sure.

Fig. 65 Old style craftsman: a tailor in Limoges.

The craftsmen

Included in 'the rest of the working population' are the self-employed craftsmen, the bookbinders, cabinet-makers, blacksmiths, who are typical French individualists, often working in pokey backstreet premises or in village barns. But they are decreasing in number as factory-made goods take over.

The professional classes

Another group in 'the rest of the working population' consists of the lawyers, doctors, and teachers, who belong to *les professions libérales*. You add *libérales* because *profession* on its own means 'work', 'job'.

Les Cadres

Cadre is a word much used nowadays. It was originally borrowed from the army, where the 'other ranks', i.e. ordinary soldiers, were called *la troupe*, and everybody else in the ranking system came into various *cadres*. Now *les cadres* refer to executives or managers of all kinds. *Les cadres moyens* are executives or managers with some sort of higher education; *les cadres supérieurs* are high-powered executives, probably possessing a second degree and possibly having been to one of the famous *Grandes Écoles* (see p. 89). The *cadres supérieurs* hold very responsible positions, are paid a high salary and enjoy the status of a professional man. Job vacancies for managers and civil servants in the columns of newspapers are classified under the heading of *Cadre*.

The employers' organization

Most workers have a union to belong to if they want to; some do not. The boss – *le patron* – also has his organization, *le Conseil National du Patronat Français*, or C.N.P.F., which corresponds to the Confederation of British Industry (C.B.I.). French employers had a bad reputation with Resistance fighters during World War II for collaborating with the Germans when France was an occupied country. So, after the liberation in 1944, the employers' national union was dissolved. The Renault car firm, which was said to have been most guilty of collaboration with the enemy, was taken over by the State and nationalized.

The C.N.P.F. was then set up in 1946. It is a confederation of various management organizations, some representing large firms, and others small factory-owners who are themselves struggling to survive in the changing industrial society where so often bigness counts. Like the craftsmen, the small farmers and the redundant worker, the small factory-owner in a provincial backwater struggles on, an individualist, hesitant about merging or moving his business.

The French working woman

Rather surprisingly, the percentage of women in France who go out to work has not changed much in the last 100 years. But the kind of work they do has changed and is changing a good deal. It used to be the uneducated women from the lowest-paid families who were forced to work for their living at so-called unskilled jobs in agriculture, housework and low-grade industrial employment. Nowadays many of the most highly educated French women take it for granted that they will work, whether they are rich or married or both. Here is the proportion of women at work in France in 1973, compared with the total working population:

Total Working Population in 1973 = $21\frac{1}{2}$ million	
Working Women = $8\frac{1}{2}$ million	

102

Increasingly women have shifted out of factories and fields into the third group of workers, into the service industries, commerce, banks, insurance offices and welfare work.

À travail égal salaire égal

Equal pay for equal work, and equal job opportunity, says French law, but in practice it doesn't work out that way in spite of repeated government attempts to strengthen the law. Women still earn up to 34 per cent less for doing the same job as men; women in top executive jobs are the greatest sufferers.

1972 Total working population   21,000,000
     Women workers   7,700,000
     Women workers = 36.2% of all workers
1974 Women workers = 37% of all workers
$\frac{2}{3}$ of women workers are on the basic minimum wage (S.M.I.C. – see p. 96)

There is still prejudice among employers, as in most Western countries, against considering a woman for some kinds of work. Sometimes they think she is not physically strong enough or hasn't the right mental equipment for a particular kind of job. In other parts of the world society has quite a different attitude to what is suitable work for women.

La femme dans la société*

Summary of research into the attitudes of French men and women as to what jobs are suitable for women.

Question asked in survey: Do you think a woman would be as good as a man in the following jobs?

Job	Percentage of those interviewed who answered 'Yes', she would be as good
1. taxi driver	59%
2. engineer	62%
3. ambassador	59%
4. industrialist	46%
5. minister in the government	45%
6. electrician	38%
7. Air-France pilot	27%
8. fitter	26%
9. surgeon	23%
10. mechanic	18%

---

*Title of book written by M-J and P-H Chombart de Lauwe, published by the Centre Nationale de la Recherche Scientifique.

Since French women were given the vote in 1944 they have slowly broken into political life. At the time of going to press there were 2 women in the Government, the Minister of Health (see p. 25) and the Secretary of State for the Welfare of Women.

Part-time work for women does not seem to be very easily available in France. This cuts down the numbers who can go out to earn while their children are young. But things are going to change; according to a survey made in 1973 there was a rise in the number of women aged between 25 and 35 going out to work, perhaps because the modern Frenchwoman has often completed her family by the time she is 28. By 1975 the percentage of all women between 25 and 54 who worked outside the home was 53 per cent. Maybe real equality of opportunity will be achieved in the land of *Liberté, Egalité, Fraternité.* After all, that slogan stands for the hopes of the French Republic, and is still to be seen on the walls of official buildings – it was originally adopted in 1793 by the French revolutionaries.

Immigrant Workers
Like other countries of Western Europe, France needs immigrant workers if her economy is to continue to expand, because there are more jobs for both skilled and unskilled workers than French men and women to fill them. The 1971–75 Government Plan for the economy – *le Sixième Plan* – allowed for an increase of 600,000 foreign workers. Things may well change, however, if the world trade recession continues and fewer workers are required.

In 1972 France had 3,400,000 immigrant workers who came mainly from the following countries

750,000	Algeria
650,000	Portugal
590,000	Italy
110,000	Morocco
95,000	Tunisia
60,000	West Africa

The state-owned Renault car factories employed a total work force of

85,000 in *1972*
95,000 in *1973*

The origin of the *unskilled workers* in these factories in 1972 was as follows:

38.5%	French
40.0%	from North Africa
14.0%	from other European countries
6.0%	from Black Africa

Immigrant workers often live in bad conditions, especially in *bidonvilles* – see p. 33 – and in cellars, and large garages. Somewhat better living conditions are to be found in hostels specially allocated to immigrants and large purpose-built residential housing blocks. The need to employ immigrant labour in France brings with it some well-known problems:

1. The language barrier; this is a relatively minor problem, because many immigrants come from former French colonies, e.g. Algeria, Senegal, where French is still spoken.
2. The cultural barrier; the Arab or African peasant from the land has a different mode of behaviour and attitude to work, when he arrives in a factory in France, from that of his European fellow-worker.
3. Tense labour relations; the French worker and trade unions can be suspicious of immigrant workers depressing wage-levels and putting up with poor working conditions.

The French government accepts responsibility for immigrant workers. In 1958 it set up a fund – *Fonds d'action sociale* (*F.A.S.*) – which advances money for housing and settling immigrants. In 1971 it granted loans of 134 million francs, about £13 million.

Illegal immigration

For a foreigner to get a job in France, in theory he needs a work-permit from the National Immigration Office. In practice the majority of immigrants have been entering the country illegally for years. With France's long land boundaries it is simple just to walk across the frontier. But if you slip in, possibly because you get fed up with waiting for French bureaucracy to provide your permit, you are likely to be at the mercy of employers who will only give you an unskilled job and pay below union wages. You won't get any rights to welfare or assistance either. You can't afford to protest for fear of losing your job, and you may fall out with your French fellow-workers, members of trade unions, who may accuse you of depressing their wages. It's not at all a comfortable position to be in.

8. Social Security – help when needed

France lost 1,400,000 men in World War I and 600,000 in World War II. It is not only the number of people killed during a war which brings down the total population figures. The fact that the dead don't produce families which in turn don't produce families another generation later, has a snow ball effect in reverse. Since the last war the government has tried to encourage its citizens to have large families – *des familles nombreuses* – to raise the French birth-rate. Quite apart from family allowances, which are the main source of help and a right under Social Security – *la Sécurité Sociale* – there are other ways of making a large number of children into a paying proposition to their parents. There are special housing allowances, big reductions in the price of rail travel, paid maternity leave for working mothers before and after the birth of a child, and financial help with day-nursery and home care for the new-born child. A father has even the right to three days' paid leave from work, called *congé de naissance*, when his wife has a baby. While it seems that a very large family of children can often be the reason for poverty in many countries, in France the large family has real advantages.

La Sécurité Sociale was set up in 1945 after the end of the war. The system was – and is – a bit complicated, because it included some pre-war national insurance schemes. But in 1945 a brand-new welfare principle was introduced; from then on every French citizen had a right to *un minimum vital*, to basic subsistence. At first the right applied only to workers and their families.

Article I of the French Social Security Act, 1945. *L'organisation de la Sécurité Sociale garantit les travailleurs et leurs familles contre les risques de toute nature susceptibles de réduire ou de supprimer leur capacité de gain* [depriving them of their earning capacity]. *Elle couvre également les charges de maternité et les charges de famille.*

Then in 1946 the social-security principle was extended. A law was passed saying: *L'assurance est obligatoire pour tous les Français, salariés ou non.* This meant that everybody had to pay national insurance contributions and that the wealthier classes who themselves wouldn't benefit much from the scheme were now paying towards the benefits that lower income groups were entitled to (see p. 108–9). It was a bit of social justice, bringing with it some redistribution of wealth.

Social Security in France deals with

Sickness,
Death   } *benefits*
and
Maternity

Retirement
and   } *pensions*
Disablement

Family   } *allowances*
                including *Housing*
Workmen's *compensation*

You will notice that unemployment benefit has not been mentioned so far. That is because it can come from two different sources; (1) from private insurance schemes, *l'Assurance chômage*, to which employers and employees contribute, under State supervision; and (2) from public funds, *l'Assistance au chômage*, for the unemployed whose income is too low, or who are 'out of benefit'. *L'Agence Nationale pour l'Emploi* – an organization of employment exchanges for matching jobs to people – is relatively new, and by all accounts is not yet working as well as had been hoped.

The French social-security system is very complicated, partly because it consists of various agencies. They have different rules and regulations, sometimes requiring so many certificates and pieces of paper from applicants for benefit that it is a wonder that some people manage to obtain what is due to them.

Fig. 66 *Guide de L'Assuré Social.*

GUIDE
de l'ASSURÉ SOCIAL

Contributions

Total contribution of employer + employee = *35% of the employee's salary*.
The State only *contributes* from taxes *11%* of all social security money paid
out *in 1970*, for example.
The scheme tries to be self-supporting.

Detailed break-down of contributions

28.5% of an employee's salary is what the *employer* has to contribute; of
this,
11.5% is for sickness, maternity and death benefits,
5.5% is for retirement pensions,
11.5% is for family allowances.
6.5% of his salary is contributed by *the employee*; of this,
3.5% is for sickness, etc.,
3.0% is for retirement pension.

Total contribution = 35%

The employer contributes to a workmen's compensation fund according
to the amount of accident risk of the particular job.

Benefits

*Distributed by the Caisse Nationale de la Sécurité Sociale and its local
branches*

Sickness benefit
   (i) A cash allowance is made for loss of earnings due to sickness for a
       period up to three years.
  (ii) Repayment is made to the sick person of 75% of doctor's fees,
       70% to 90% of prescription charges, and 80% of hospital charges.
Miners and railway workers get free treatment at present.

The National Health Service in France does not operate in the same
way as in Britain. The *Sécurité Sociale* fixes the scale of doctors' fees.
However, there are more 'private' doctors outside the N.H.S. in France
than in the U.K, and they do not have a contract with the *Sécurité Sociale*
fixing their scale of fees. Patients can go to any doctor, private or N.H.S.,
but can only claim a refund of the fixed charges. As 'private' doctors charge
more than the registered Social Security ones, you have to watch out when
you need medical attention in France or you may find yourself seriously
out of pocket.

Another snag is that the patient has to pay the doctor before claiming
a refund on the fees – which may mean a wait of a week or more before
you get your money back.

Hospitals want to know where payment is coming from before you are
admitted, except in cases of emergency. The Social Security transfers the

benefit due to you directly to some hospitals. At others the patient pays and claims the money back. For those who can't afford to pay there is *L'Aide Sociale* (see p. 111).

Retirement Pensions

(i)   They are based on the number of years you have contributed to the *Sécurité Sociale*,
(ii) and also on the best ten years' salary or wages you earned in your working life.
(iii) Any French citizen aged 65 or over has the right to a basic pension, whether he is an ex-wage-earner or not.

The French government has promised to introduce pensions for all at 60.

Family Allowances

They are paid to any household with more than one child – a 'child' being a person under 18, or under 20 if still continuing education.

Un salaire unique is a supplement paid if there is only a single minimum income coming in to a family. The allowance varies according to the number of children, their age, and place of residence.

Sociétés Mutualistes

In addition to the State social-security schemes there are many Friendly Societies still in existence in France. Until recently they were called *Sociétés Mutuelles*, or *Mutuelles* for short. They were founded by workmen – and not only in France – in a great self-help movement in the nineteenth century before the Welfare State was ever thought of. Recently, too, a number of supplementary pension schemes have been worked out between the trade unions and employers to top up State pensions.

Special Welfare Schemes

Holidays for all – Special Welfare Schemes

There are subsidized holidays for families who could not otherwise afford to go away.

There are federations of non-profit-making establishments which provide an enormous choice of holidays for the whole family at cheap rates, often with support from government, local or school funds: Fédération des Maisons Familiales de Vacances, and Fédération des Villages et Camping Familiaux de Vacances.

Fig. 67 Holidays for all.

For your holidays you can choose between hotels, guest-houses, holiday camps, and camping sites, and you pay according to your means. If your means are slender you may get your holiday free.

Children's holidays are specially catered for, over and above the family party. Municipalities run their own *colonies de vacances* or place their pupils in a *colonie* run by the *Union française des Centres de Vacances et de Loisirs* (U.F.O.V.). The Union has a day when it collects money from the public to help run its 3,000 holiday centres. It reminds the general public that the lucky 1½ million children and adolescents who had a holiday in one of the Union's centres were only a half of all those who could have benefited if there had been enough money and places for them.

Still, France seems to be taking holidays for the underprivileged very seriously. Special arrangements are being made for old-age pensioners to go to holiday camps free of charge during May and June, the off-peak season.

L'aide sociale

It has to be remembered that *la Sécurité Sociale* is intended to be self-supporting: it is an insurance system in which contributions should cover benefits. But there will always be occasions in any community when people are 'out of benefit', fall on hard times, or have incomes too low to pay the percentage of medical expenses and so on not covered by Social Security. *L'Aide Sociale* may come to their help; it is community aid directly descended from the charitable institutions and Public Assistance of former days. In theory *l'Aide Sociale* is supposed to wither away, as insurance should cover the whole of the population in time. At present the money comes from government, *département* (County Council), and municipal funds. Those in need apply at the Town Hall and their case is considered by a committee. In an emergency, for example hospital admittance, the mayor makes a decision which is later reviewed by the committee. If they decide against you, you are liable for all expenses involved. But presumably you applied for aid in the first place because you hadn't the money!

9. News and Views – the mass media

Broadcasting

Radio and television used to be run by an organization called O.R.T.F.: you pronounced each letter, as in B.B.C. The letters stood for *Office de Radiodiffusion-Télévision Française.*

Broadcasting was centrally controlled and the director-general was directly responsible to the Minister of Information. People grew worried about rumours of government interference in the programmes put out on radio and television, so, in times of crisis (for example, during the events of May 1968) they tended to listen to stations broadcasting from across the frontiers of France in order to get what they hoped was reliable news. In order to sort matters out and to break the monopoly, O.R.T.F. was reorganized into divisions in 1975 with Radio France and each of the three Television Channels working independently and in competition with one another. The *stations périphériques* around the edge of France – Radio Luxembourg, Europe N° 1, Radio Monte Carlo, and Sud-Radio – are still popular. They are run by commercial companies based outside France, but even they are not entirely independent. The French government holds a substantial number of shares in the companies, allows some of them to work from offices and studios in Paris, and permits the erection of relay-masts on French soil. So the government can exert some pressure on the foreign companies.

Whatever French people may think about the reliability of television and radio news, they are as keen as any other nation on gluing their eyes to the screen in search of entertainment. But opinion polls have shown that if dad and mum are keen, their kids are not quite so. According to a survey, *la télévision semble intégrée à la vie de famille, et 54% des jeunes gens interrogé déclarent quitter la salle commune aussitôt après le repas, pour éviter la soirée devant l'écran. Les jeunes gens*, those aged between 13 and 20, tend to listen to the radio because it gives them a chance of choosing their own programme and listening on their own. Radio forms a kind of defence against parents too, and reinforces the young people's privacy. The radio keeps them up to date with what's new in records, and so listening is a kind of youth-group activity.

Newspapers and magazines

The French are not so obsessed with reading newspapers as the British, so circulation figures are not so high as in the U.K. The French buy only

---

• • • LE MONDE — 19 septembre 1975 — Page 17

RADIO-TÉLÉVISION

LES PROGRAMMES

« Le Monde » publie tous les samedis, numéro daté du dimanche-lundi, un supplément radio - télévision avec les programmes complets de la semaine.

JEUDI 18 SEPTEMBRE

CHAINE I : **TF 1**

20 h. 35 (R.), Série : **Salvator et les Mohicans de Paris**, d'après A. Dumas , mise en scène B. Borderie ; avec R. Etcheverry ; 21 h. 25, **Les dossiers d'IT l : Houari Boumediène** (co-production « le Monde »-Seuil audiovisuel).
22 h. 25, **Allons au cinéma**, d'A. Halimi ; 23 h., IT 1 dernière.

CHAINE II (couleur) : **A 2**

20 h. 30, Dramatique : « **Anne-Marie ou quelque chose d'autre** »; réal. M. Failevic ; scénario M. Failevic et A. Mignard ; avec H. Duc. J.-P. Bagot

L'échec d'un couple évoqué au moment de la « conciliation » qui précède le divorce. Ou comment l'usure quotidienne peut mener au crime passionnel.
22 h., Magazine de variétés : **Vous avez dit bizarre...**, de M. Lancelot ; 22 h. 45, Journal de l'A 2.

CHAINE III (couleur) : **FR 3**

20 h. 30, Un film, un auteur : « le Vice et la

Vertu », de R. Vadim (1962) ; avec A. Girardot, R. Hossein. C. Deneuve, O. E. Hasse, Ph. Lemaire (N.).

Pendant l'été 44, alors que sa sœur Juliette devient la maîtresse et la complice d'un colonel S.S., la douce et pure Justine est déportée dans un château tyrolien pour servir, avec d'autres filles, les plaisirs d'une société érotique de nazis.
22 h. 10, FR 3 Actualités.

FRANCE-CULTURE

20 n., Carte blanche, de L. Siou : « le Temps des Russes », de W. Kirchner, adapt L. Richard, avec L. Lemercier, R. Favey, N. Nerval, B. Lange. J. Brassat, réal. Horowicz ; 21 n. 13, Disques ; 21 n 40 (R.). « Hector. Arthur, Edgar Dupont » de M. Cassan, réal. C. Roland-Manuel ; 22 h. 30 (R.), Entretien avec Marcel Duchamp ; 23 h., De la nuit ; 23 h. 50, Poésie.

FRANCE-MUSIQUE

20 h. 5 (S.) Les bons mouvements ; 20 h. 30 (S.), Orchestre national, dir. H. Scherchen : « Cinquième symphonie en do dièse mineur » (Mahler) ; 22 h. 30 (S.), Les symphonistes français (Bizet, Honegger, Charpentier) ; 24 h. (S.), Plans sur plans, par Eric Dietlin.

VENDREDI 19 SEPTEMBRE

CHAINE I : **TF 1**

20 h. 35, Au théâtre ce soir : « **Il etait une gare** », de J. Deval, mise en scène de J Mauclair. Avec R. Faure, J Marin. J. Mauclair.

Seize habitués du rail échouent, par les hasards du « transit forcé ». sur le quai d'une petite gare.
22 h. 25, Variétés : **Le Club de dix heures**, de J. Chabannes ; 22 h. 55, IT 1 dernière.

CHAINE II (couleur) : **A 2**

20 h. 30, Série : **Benjowski** (5e épisode) ; 21 h. 30, Emission littéraire : **Apostrophes**, (les révolutionnaires) ; 22 h. 35, Ciné-club : « **le Dahlia bleu** », de G. Marshall (1946). Avec A. Ladd, V. Lake, W. Bendix, H. de Silva.

En 1945, à Los Angeles, un ancien pilote, qui vient d'être démobilisé, est soupçonné d'avoir tué sa femme infidèle. Il cherche à découvrir le véritable meurtrier.
0 h. 10, **Journal de l'A 2.**

CHAINE III (couleur) : **FR 3**

20 h. 30, Documentaire : **Civilisation**, de Sir Kennets Clark (**le romanesque et la réalité**) ;
21 h. 20, **Toutes les villes sont mortelles : Tanger. ville ouverte, ville masquee**. Réal. E. Sarsini ; 22 h. 10, FR 3 actualités.

FRANCE-CULTURE

20 h. (S.), « **Xerxes** ». de Haendel, avec L. Devos, E. Brunner, J. Chamonin, C. Wirz, P.-Ch. Runge, P.-M. Pegaud, J. Bona orchestre de chambre de Radio-France et chœurs Jean-Baptiste Lully ; direct. B. Amaducci ; 22 h. 30 (R.). Entretien avec Marcel Duchamp ; 23 h, De la nuit.

FRANCE-MUSIQUE

20 h. 5 (S.), Les bons mouvements ; 20 h. 30 (S.), Orchestre national, direct. L. Bernstein Hommage à Ravel : « Alborada de Gracioso » ; « Schéhérazade » ; « Concerto en sol » ; « Tzigane » ; « la Valse » ; 22 h. 30 (S.), Les symphonistes français (Lalo, d'Indy) ; 24 h. (S.), Concert pour mon chat.

Fig. 68 A selection of television programmes.

half as many daily papers as the British, and come eighteenth in the world league table of newspaper addicts. There are not many French newspapers published on Sundays, so there is nothing to compare with the 6 million circulation of the *News of the World*, which has the largest circulation of any newspaper in Britain. On the other hand, judging from the range of weeklies and magazines to be found on the counters of newsagents in France, there must be plenty of keen newsprint-readers in general.

If you want a daily newspaper delivered to your door you have to pay a subscription, and then the paper is sent to you through the post. There aren't any newspaper delivery boys or girls in France. If you don't pay a subscription you can buy your copy at the kiosk in the street, at a *tabac* – a bar licensed to sell stamps – or at a *librairie* – a bookseller's. The trouble with a subscription is that you can't easily stop the paper when you go away from home, so it is easier to buy as you go.

Fig. 69 Kiosk or news stand in Paris.

Paris or the provinces?

In spite of the importance of Paris, Paris daily papers don't dominate the scene throughout the country. Even the ones with an international reputation sell a relatively small number of copies.

THE PARIS PAPERS

Le Monde	Le Figaro	France-Soir	L'Humanité
No pictures	Rather conservative	Has largest circulation	The official French Communist Party paper
Small print	Runs small and many property-for-sale advertisements	Goes in for banner head-lines	Has little advertising, but its opinions carry weight with its rather older readership
Aimed at the intelligent reader	Not so shaky financially as some papers are	Is an evening paper with the next day's date on it	
Full of articles *about* the news			
Comes out in the afternoon under the next day's date			

Approximate Daily circulation 1975
432,000   402,000   727,000(1974)   151,000

SPACE GIVEN DURING ONE WEEK IN 1974 TO	LE MONDE	LE FIGARO	FRANCE-SOIR
HOME AFFAIRS	5·7%	4·9%	5·3%
FOREIGN AFFAIRS	13·3%	8 6%	4·2%
ECONOMIC AND FINANCIAL AFFAIRS	14·3%	7·4%	19·0%
LEISURE	2·3%	3·3%	4·9%
EDUCATION	1·8%	0·8%	0·2%
SPORT	1·8%	4·7%	0·2%
TV, RADIO, THEATRE, THE ARTS	9·3%	8·8%	11·5%
LITERATURE	4·4%	3·1%	0·8%
SCIENCE AND MEDICINE	2·8%	0·7%	0·4%
GENERAL INFORMATION	5·9%	9·1%	10·9%
ADVERTISEMENTS	38·4%	48·6%	49·2%

Chine populaire, *La Chine communiste*, *La Chine Rouge*, or *La République populaire chinoise*. You can influence attitudes by your choice of words, by the headlines in your paper, by the pictures and the captions under them that you print. Suppose for example that there were newspaper reports about the same man involved in 2 different incidents. This is how they might read:

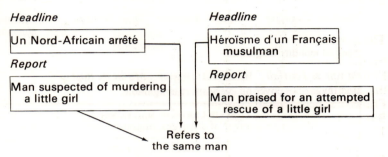

The freedom of the French press has been helped by associations of editorial staffs – *les sociétés des rédacteurs*. In 1951 the staff of *Le Monde* formed an association to counter outside interference with what they were writing and printing. *Le Monde* has a high reputation, and it has encouraged other papers, for example *Le Figaro* and *Ouest-France*, to follow its lead. The editorial staffs have to try to keep their own 'houses' in order.

10. Politics in France – How France is Run

The system

France is a republic.
France has a written Constitution which lays down the rules for running the country.
France has been a republic continuously since 1870, and twice before that.
But the Constitution has changed from time to time.
The present Constitution was adopted in 1958.

Constitution du 4 Octobre 1958.

Art.2 – La France est une République indivisible, laïque, démocratique et sociale. Elle assure l'égalité devant la loi de tous les citoyens sans distinction d'origine, de race ou de religion. Elle respecte toutes les croyances.

L'emblème national est le drapeau tricolore, bleu, blanc, rouge.

L'hymne national est la 'Marseillaise'.

La devise de la République est 'Liberté, Egalité, Fraternité.'

Son principe est: gouvernement du peuple, par le peuple et pour le peuple.

A Short Constitutional History of France since the eighteenth century

1789	End of the Ancien Régime – the old form of government Declaration of the Rights of Man	
1792	Execution of King Louis XVI, a Bourbon. Proclamation of the ———————→	FIRST REPUBLIC
1804	Napoleon Bonaparte proclaimed Emperor	THE EMPIRE
1815	Fall of Napoleon Restoration of Bourbon Kings	MONARCHY
1830	July Revolution Louis Philippe, another Bourbon, proclaimed King MONARCHY	
1848	Revolution Proclamation of the ———————→	SECOND REPUBLIC
1851	Louis Bonaparte seizes power	
1852	Louis Bonaparte proclaimed Emperor	SECOND EMPIRE

| 1870 | Defeat of French army in the Franco-Prussian War leads to end of Second Empire
Proclamation of the ⟶ | THIRD REPUBLIC |

1940   Occupation of France by Hitler's German forces. General Pétain sets up a French Government in Vichy, General de Gaulle is head of the Free French Forces in London.

1944   Liberation of France from the Germans

| 1946 | Republican Constitution adopted ⟶ | FOURTH REPUBLIC |

| 1958 | Uprising in Algeria.
Parliamentary crisis.
New Constitution adopted in October ⟶ | FIFTH REPUBLIC |

1959   de Gaulle takes office as President in January

Down the ladder of the French Government

President	*le Président de la République*
Prime Minister	*le Président du Conseil des Ministres*
Cabinet	*le Conseil de Ministres*
Parliament consisting of	*le Parlement*
The National Assembly	*l'Assemblée Nationale*
The Senate	*le Sénat*
District Councils	*les Conseils Généraux*
Local Councils	*les Conseils Municipaux*

The President is the head of the Republic. He holds office for seven years. He is elected by a simple majority of all the votes cast by the registered native French voters in the special presidential election.

The President of the Republic, as well as being head of State, is also head of the French government. He presides over the Council of Ministers. It is as though the King or Queen of England presided at Cabinet meetings, as well as being the formal head of State who receives ambassadors and hands out medals at the Palace.

Not only does the President guide the Council of Ministers, he also chooses the Prime Minister. During de Gaulle's 'reign' he didn't even worry whether the Prime Minister was acceptable to a majority of members of Parliament. Yet it is Parliament which passes the laws determining the way the country is run. If the Prime Minister can't get a majority of MPs to vote for his proposals there is deadlock. It must be said that at present the President is careful to choose an acceptable Prime Minister, but in his day de Gaulle felt so sure of himself and of the French voters that if there was deadlock he simply threatened to dissolve Parliament, to resign, or to hold a referendum.

If a President of the Fifth Republic wants to refer a question over the head of Parliament direct to the voters, he can call for a referendum; a simple question is put and a simple answer given – Yes or No. You can see that it depends a bit on how and when the question is asked as to what answer comes back. The referendum – even the threat of one – is a powerful weapon in Presidential hands. In many cases it boils down to: 'Do you prefer them (Parliament) or me?'

The French Parliament

consists of *two Houses*,

The National Assembly with 487 members called *députés* elected for five years by all French citizens over 18 years old.
It sits at the *Palais Bourbon* in Paris.

The Senate with 279 senators elected for nine years by the National Assembly deputies and delegates from local councils.
It sits at the *Palais du Luxembourg* in Paris.

The President's official residence is the *Elysée* Palace.

When you look at the French political system you can't help being impressed by the importance of the President compared with the Parliament or Ministers. Because the President is the Head of State he is not to be criticized or called to account by Parliament for his actions. So it has been said that deputies have lost their real responsibility for the way France is run.

It is partly their own fault. Between 1945 and 1958, the year de Gaulle took over, the average length of life of a French government was six months. To a great extent this was due to the large number of political parties in France. To exert any influence splinter groups and small parties had to come to some arrangement to support each other if their ideas were remotely similar. Such arrangements didn't generally last long once a government was formed, because differences between the parties soon reappeared.

In 1958 a crisis developed. The overseas territory of Algeria was struggling for independence from France. There was war abroad and terrorism at home. One government after another was unable to cope with the situation so the then President of the Republic called on the 'strong man' of the nation to take command, and Parliament confirmed de Gaulle in office by 329 votes to 224. Thus the Fifth Republic was born.

121

Fig. 70 The President and Mme de Gaulle on a state visit to London.

'Moi, le général de Gaulle'[1]

Although he is now dead and a part of history, you can see why it is impossible to understand France today without knowing a little about de Gaulle.

Born 1890
Leader of Free French Forces in London 1940–44
Head of the Provisional French Government in Paris 1944–45
Retired to his country house to write his memoirs
Recalled to save France from threatened upheaval – Algerian crisis 1958
President of the French Republic December 1958–April 1969
Retired to his country house to finish his memoirs
Died 1970

If de Gaulle came in in 1958 to settle a restless country, he almost went out in 1968 when revolt was again in the air. The French refer to this period as 'the events of May 1968' – *les événements*. Student revolts broke out in Paris at the Nanterre University campus. The riot police, called the *C.R.S.*, – *Compagnies Républicaines de Sécurité* – were sent to quell the students. Their methods were rough. Soon full-scale battles were raging in the streets of Paris, barricades were thrown up in the *Quartier Latin*, cobblestones were torn up and used as ammunition against the hated *C.R.S.*, cars were overturned and set on fire. The spirit of revolution was in the air and the revolt spread to other universities, schools, and factories. People were demonstrating that they were fed up with authority, with tradition, with 'them'.

Ordinary life came to a standstill. Students tried to link up with factory-workers, who went on strike. It looked like the end of de Gaulle and the

[1] In speeches General de Gaulle always referred to himself as 'I, General de Gaulle'.

Fig. 71 The C.R.S., May 1968. With rifles reversed, to be used as clubs, riot police start a charge against students.

Fifth Republic. But after two or three weeks de Gaulle had ridden out the storm. He was still in office and his Ministers were promising reforms. Yet a year later he had resigned and today there is not much evidence of reform. So who won?

The 'reign' of de Gaulle and the events of May 1968 certainly left their mark on France. De Gaulle stood for tradition, patriotism, *la gloire*, the glorious past of France to be continued into the present. When he had to solve problems he would often finally give way in order to stay in power. For rebellious Frenchmen this was not enough. France has a history of revolution going back over almost two hundred years. What many Frenchmen still say they want is change.

Fig. 72 The National Assembly in session.

The French political parties

Of the political parties working for change the French Communist Party
– *P.C.F.* – was and still is the strongest single party. It attracts many different types, not only the workers but property-owning middle-class
people and especially the intellectuals, writers, painters, actors. They
will support it in 'demos' and vote for it in elections.

There are other parties working for change, namely a number of different kinds of Socialists; they hope to make common cause with the
Communists in a United Front.

The parties which supported General de Gaulle grouped themselves
into the *Union des Démocrates pour la République – U.D.R.* The Union
continues to be the voice of French conservative opinion.

Then there are the moderates, who may want to change things gradually.
They include parties like the *Mouvement réformateur – Réf.*

When they have been elected and take their places in the National
Assembly, the deputies sit in a semicircle.

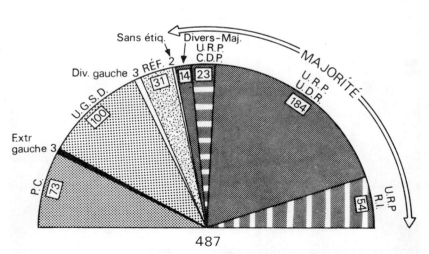

Fig. 73 The National Assembly: distribution of seats according to parties in the
semi-circular Chamber of the Palais-Bourbon after the election of March, 1973.

124

Key to Fig. 73, reading from left to right

P.C.	*Parti communiste*	Communist Party
Extr. gauche	*Extrême gauche*	Far Left parties
U.G.S.D.	*Union de la gauche socialiste et démocrate*	Union of the Socialists and Democrats of the Left
Div. gauche	*Divers gauche*	Various leftists
Réf.	*Mouvement réformateur*	Reform Movement
Sans étiqu.	*Sans étiquette*	Independents
Divers maj.	*Divers majorité*	Various M.P.s voting with the majority, supporting the government
U.R.P./C.D.P.	*Union des Républicains de Progrès/ Centre Démocratique et Progrès*	Union of Progressive Republicans in alliance with the Democratic and Progressive Centre Party
U.R.P./U.D.R.	*Union des Républicains de Progrès/ Union des Droites pour la République*	Union of Progressive Republicans in alliance with the Union of the Right for the Republic
U.R.P./R.I.	*Union des Républicains de Progrès/ Républicains Indépendants*	Union of Progressive Republicans in alliance with the Independent Republicans

Although after subsequent elections the number of representatives of each party is likely to alter and the alliances made between different groups in the Assembly may change, a range of political opinion from Left to Right is likely to remain. Of course, the majority of deputies supporting the government may alter too, perhaps moving more to the Centre or to the Left. They arrange themselves roughly in blocks, with the U.D.R. on the right, the Communists and Socialists on the left, and the moderate Centre parties in between.

At all stages along the line the politicians will be making new agreements with each other and moving into different groups, which may even suddenly appear under a new name.

The result for everybody, including the French public, is very confusing.

No wonder that French people do not belong to political parties to the same extent as the British do.

In Britain 1 person in every 5 is a member of a political party.
In France 1 person in every 35 is a member of a political party.

Some possible reasons: (1) the French are 'non-joiners' by nature; (2) the trade unions are not tied to political parties and therefore not geared to signing up party members (3) the French tend to be 'against' a political party rather than 'for' one – at least this shows up when they vote in elections, if they even bother to register to vote.

The French voting system

There are 30 million people who may vote in France.
Voting takes place in constituencies.

Fig. 74 Which shall I vote for? Parliamentary Elections, Marly-le-Roi, Yvelines.

Each voter has one vote.
He/she has a list of candidates to choose from.
There may be as many as 11 candidates on the list, each from a different political party.
A voter usually has to vote twice, because there is a first ballot on one Sunday and a second a week later.
First ballot: to be elected, a candidate has to get the majority of the votes cast plus at least a quarter of the votes of all voters on the register.
If no candidate succeeds in this, then there is a Second Ballot: to be elected, a candidate now only needs a simple majority over all other candidates.

You can imagine the bargaining that goes on behind the scenes during the week between the two ballots. Candidates who got relatively few votes on the first Sunday are under pressure to withdraw because their cause is hopeless. Or there may be a 'carve-up' behind the scenes; a candidate's party may have made a pre-election arrangement with another party having rather similar policies, to support whichever candidate stands the better chance in the second ballot. So the list of candidates is thinned out for Ballot No. 2. But in many cases the object of an agreement between parties to support each other may simply be to keep a third party's candidate out.

So this is the way the Constitution of the Fifth Republic works: the President has his own election for office and a great deal of power; Parliament is elected under an elaborate system and tends to be ineffective; the Prime Minister is a kind of superior messenger between the two.

The result is that the average Frenchman feels he has no influence on

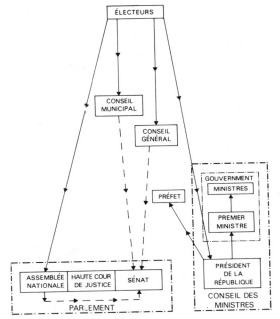

Fig. 75 *Les différents pouvoirs politiques de la Ve République.*

the way his country is run, at least not via his elected representatives.

There is one minor way in which he may be able to make his voice heard. The Constitution provides for an Economic and Social Planning Council.

Le Conseil Économique et Social

The Council has to be consulted by the government about any law it wants to pass or any project it is planning which has to do with economic or social matters. It is made up of

200 members
80 nominated by the government, and
120 nominated by associations of professional and social workers and by the trade unions.

Among these 120 there should be someone to speak up for the interests of the salaried worker and wage-earner – even if they are only being consulted.

Local Government

The French citizen also has a vote to elect representatives to the local council, *Le Conseil Municipal*, which deals with matters concerning his

Fig. 76 *Conseil municipal à Montenay, Mayenne.*

home area – *la commune*. Here *M. le Maire* is the important public servant, ruling the roost from the *Mairie* or Town Hall, which even the smallest municipality has. But oddly enough, Paris has a different system and no mayor.

There is also a district council to be elected, *Le Conseil Géneral*, which deals with matters concerning the *département*, much as a large County Council would in Britain.

M. le Préfet is the government's representative in the *département*, and he is the link-man between Paris and the local councils.

The influence of government

You get the impression that the French are kept quite as busy as any citizens of any modern democracy at electing various layers of government. What does the government in Paris actually do when it is elected? How does the Frenchman-in-the-street *feel* the influence of government?

This is where he will feel it:

Taxes – national and local; VAT on the goods he buys; car and petrol taxes

Inflation –   prices rising faster than wages
Call-up for military service
Education   Welfare services (see p. 106–111)

Nationalized industries or enterprises, for example,

Electricity	*Electricité de France*
Gas	*Gaz de France*
Coal	*Charbonnages*
Fuel Oil	*Compagnie française des Pétroles*
Renault Car Plant	*Régie Nationale des Usines Renault*
Docks	*Ports autonomes*
Railways	*Société Nationale des Chemins de Fer* (the State owns 51 % of the shares)
Paris Airport	*Aéroport de Paris*
French Airlines	*Air-France, Air-Inter*
Aircraft Industry	*Sud-Aviation*
Radio and TV	*Radio-Télévision*
Insurance Companies	*Sociétés nationales d'assurances*
Banks	*Banque de France, Crédit Lyonnais, Société Générale*
Monopoly sale of tobacco and matches	*Service d'Exploitation Industrielle de Tabac et Allumettes*

and there are many more.

For a long time the French government has been able to intervene in private industry, buying up or investing in private businesses in part, and directing the way it wants private industry to develop. It has ways of making good the deficiencies in the public services; for instance, if there aren't enough schools it relies on private ones provided by the Church. Public servants like doctors and university professors are known to use the State-run hospitals and laboratories to treat private patients and do research for fees. The public services suffer.

The French citizen is probably not so worried about the tie-up between government and business. His concern is about the dehumanizing effects of technology, and he is afraid of being nothing more than a number in a system. He is rightly worried about French bureaucracy. The tyranny and sometimes the rudeness of minor civil servants in government offices, in the Post Office and Social Security for instance, can be infuriating. The French citizen also suspects that if you know how, have money or influence, or can do someone a good turn behind the scenes, you can usually get your own way; a property developer in France often seems to be able to get round planning laws. Now this kind of thing goes on in most countries, not only in France. But in France most particularly, and for a long time now, the attitude of the public to politicians has been: 'They are ALL corrupt.' Furthermore, for the French man-in-the-street, bureaucracy and scandal, especially about tax-evasion by the rich, seems to divide 'them' from 'us'. He mutters: 'C'est nous qui allons payer', and he resents it – but he laps up the scandals in the newspapers all the same.

11. Beyond the Boundaries of France

France and the EEC

In 1957 France was a founder-member of the European Common Market – *le Marché Commun* – expanded from six to nine participating countries in January 1973, which was when Britain entered. France has benefited from the large European market, in which she can sell her manufactures on favourable terms, largely because she has put enormous amounts of money into re-equipping and re-siting her industry. The government assists by planning the economy ahead for five-year stretches (the Sixth National Plan running from 1971 to 1975, the Seventh from 1975 to 1980) and it helps industry in ways such as granting loans for modernization. As a result the French export trade has increased because her prices are competitive.

After de Gaulle came to power in 1958 he managed to get the best out of what might seem to be a contradictory position:

    partnership with Europe

and

    emphasis on the individual nationhood of France, based on her glorious past.

France recognized after World War II that the armed struggle with Germany (involving three wars in seventy years) could not be repeated. It had exhausted the nation, and had meant that territories like Alsace and Lorraine were always being shuttled to and fro. Now there are regular meetings between German and French heads of government, and relations between the two countries have clearly improved. It looks as though their young people born after the end of the last war travel about Europe more freely than their parents, have more in common with each other than with the older generation, and are not inclined to revive bitter memories.

France's cultural connections in Europe

For centuries French was the language of the aristocracy and the educated classes on the Continent, especially in Eastern Europe, in Poland and Russia. Paris was the city to which people who could afford it went for a taste of the artistic life, for fashion and entertainment. Paris was the city which political refugees naturally made for. To a certain extent these ties still exist.

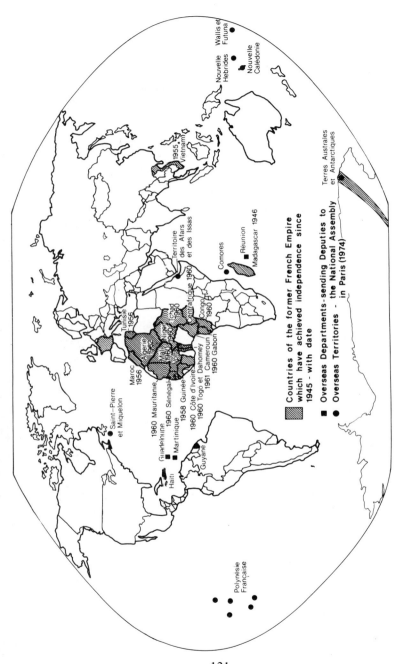

Map 12 World map showing French dependencies sending deputies to the National Assembly 1973

Wallis et Futuna

Nouvelle Hebrides

Nouvelle Caledonie

1955 Vietnam

Terres Australes et Antarctiques

Reunion 1946

Territoire des Afars et des Issas

Madagascar 1946

Comores

Centrafrique 1960

Tunisie 1956

Algerie 1962

Mali 1960

Tchad 1960

Niger 1960

Congo 1960

Gabon 1960

Maroc 1956

Cameroun 1960

1960 Mauritanie

1960 Senegal

1958 Guinee

1960 Côte d'Ivoire

1960 Togo et Dahomey

1961 Haute-Volta

Saint-Pierre et Miquelon

Guadeloupe

Martinique

Haiti

Guyane

Polynésie Française

⬛ Countries of the former French Empire which have achieved independence since 1945 - with date

■ Overseas Departments - sending Deputies to the National Assembly

● Overseas Territories - the National Assembly in Paris (1974)

131

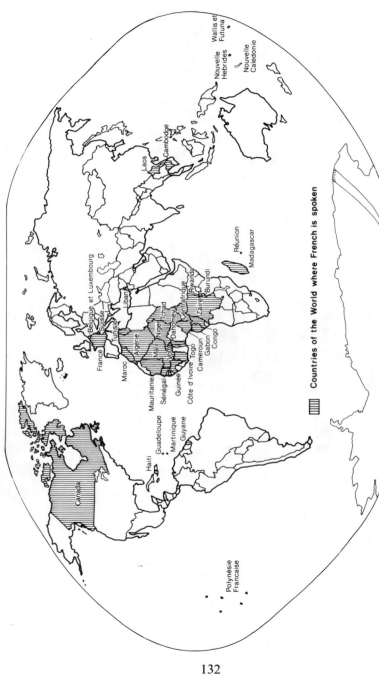

Wallis et
Futuna

Nouvelle
Hébrides

Nouvelle
Calédonie

Cambodge

Laos

Belgique et Luxembourg

Suisse

Liban

Tunisie

France

Maroc

Algérie

Mauritanie

Sénégal

Guinée

Côte d'Ivoire

Mali

Niger

Togo

Dahomey

Tchad

Centrafrique

Cameroun

Gabon

Congo

Zaïre

Rwanda

Burundi

Réunion

Madagascar

Haïti

Guadeloupe

Martinique

Guyane

Canada

Polynésie
Française

Countries of the World where French is spoken

Map 13 La France francophone

(NB. In the case of Canada, there are two official languages: French and English.)

132

French is still a major language of diplomacy. But English is increasingly taking over as the 'world language' which those in trade, government and science must know in order to get on.

La France outre-mer

If you see a list of French Parliamentary constituencies or read a newspaper report about the results of French elections, you may be reminded that France once had a great Empire overseas; for the few remaining French dependencies send deputies to sit in the National Assembly in Paris.

The right of overseas dependencies to choose independence is written into the French constitution of 1958, so their number may continue to dwindle.

Independent or not, countries overseas which were or are attached to France are likely to get preferential treatment in economic relations with the French government as far as the rules of the European Common Market permit. France likes to feel that she has a special responsibility for her former territories. After all, large or small, French is likely still to be their official language, and French is still spoken by many of their inhabitants.

France is not isolated from the rest of the world, and perhaps not so inward-looking as some people suggest. But the French are immensely patriotic and on the whole rightly so, for life in France today is, for many of her citizens, most agreeable.

Short list of abbreviations

C.E.E.	Communauté Économique Européenne
C.G.T.	Confédération Générale du Travail
C.N.R.S.	Centre Nationale de la Recherche Scientifique
C.R.S.	Compagnies Républicaines de Sécurité
E.N.A.	École Nationale d'Administration
F.M.I.	Fonds Monétaire International
H.L.M.	Habitation à Loyer Modéré
I.F.O.P.	Institut Français d'Opinion Publique
O.N.U.	Organisation des Nations Unies (U.N.)
O.R.T.F.	Office de la Radio Télévision Française
O.S.	Ouvrier Spécialisé (semi-skilled worker)
O.T.A.N.	Organisation du Traité de l'Atlantique Nord (N.A.T.O.)
P.C.	Parti Communiste
P.T.T.	Postes, Télégraphes, Téléphones
R.E.R.	Réseau Express Régional
S.M.I.C.	Salaire Minimum Interprofessionel de Croissance
S.N.C.F.	Société Nationale des Chemins de Fer Français
S.O.F.R.E.S.	Société Française d'Enquête par Sondage
T.V.A.	Taxe sur la Valeur Ajoutée (V.A.T.)

Selective Bibliography

Official publications

Documents in English obtainable from the
   Ambassade de France,
   Service de Presse et d'Information,
   58, Knightsbridge,
   London S.W.1.
   1. France Facts and Figures.
   2. News from France.

Documents in French:
Brèves Nouvelles de France, published weekly by L'Association pour la diffusion de la pensée française, Paris XV*e*.
Les Cahiers Français, Revue périodique de l'activité politique, économique, sociale et culturelle de la France, published six times a year by La Documentation Française.
Données Sociales, published by INSEE (Institut National de la Statistique et des Études Économiques) 1973.
Économie et Statistique, Revue mensuelle, published by INSEE.
France, published by La Documentation Française, Paris, 1972, in both French and English versions.
France Informations, published by the Ministère des Affaires Etrangères, (Service d'Information et de Presse), 37 Quai d'Orsay, Paris VII*e*.
Informations Sociales, Revue de l'action sociale, du travail et des collectivités, 10 issues annually; published by the Caisse Nationale des Allocations Familiales, 47 Chaussée d'Antin, Paris VI*e*.
Tendances, La France en Europe et dans le Monde, published in alternate months by L'Association pour la diffusion de la pensée française, Paris XV*e*.
1985. La France face au choc du Futur. Plan et Prospectives, issued by the Commissariat Général du Plan, published by Armand Colin 1972.

N.B.   The titles of some publications, especially hand-outs, may be changed from time to time; the publications may even be discontinued.

Other publications

L'Année politique, économique, sociale et diplomatique en France, 1971 and 1973 editions, Presses Universitaires.
Ardagh, John, *The New France. De Gaulle and After*, Pelican 1970.

Cazes, Georges, et Reynaud, Alain, *Les mutations récentes de l'économie française. De la croissance à l'aménagement*, Doin, éditeurs, Paris 1973.

Centre d'Étude et de Promotion de la Lecture, *La Pédagogie, Les problèmes, les méthodes, les enseignements, Les dictionnaires du savoir moderne*, Denoël 1972. *La Politique, Les Sciences de l'Action*, Hachette 1971.

Dupeux, Georges, *La France de 1945 a 1965*, Collection U$_2$, Armand Colin 1969.

Goguel, François, et Grosser, Alfred, *La Politique en France*, Collection U/Série 'Société Politique', Armand Colin 1964.

Gravier, J. F., *Paris et le désert français en 1972*, Flammarion 1972.

Majault, Joseph, *L'Enseignement en France,* Contemporary European Studies Series, McGraw-Hill 1973.

Parodi, M., *L'Économie et la Société Française de 1945 à 1970.* Collection U/Série 'Sciences économiques et Gestion', Armand Colin 1971.

Thompson, I. B., *Modern France. A Social and Economic Geography of France*, Butterworth 1970.

Trotignon, Yves, *La France au XXe siècle*, Collection Études Supérieures, Section Historique, Bordas-Mouton, Paris 1968.

Index

N.B.   Where there are several page references, numbers in italics indicate the main entry.

137